Eight Sessions to Help You
Discover What It Means to Follow Jesus
Together with Fellow Believers

I Am A Christian

PARTICIPANT'S GUIDE

THOM S. RAINER
WITH ASHLEY WIERSMA

TYNDALE MOMENTUM®

A Tyndale nonfiction imprint

Visit Tyndale online at tyndale.com.

Visit Tyndale Momentum online at tyndalemomentum.com.

Tyndale, Tyndale's quill logo, *Tyndale Momentum*, and the Tyndale Momentum logo are registered trademarks of Tyndale House Ministries. Tyndale Momentum is a nonfiction imprint of Tyndale House Publishers, Carol Stream, Illinois.

I Am a Christian Participant's Guide: Eight Sessions to Help You Discover What It Means to Follow Jesus Together with Fellow Believers

Designed by Eva M. Winters

For information about special discounts for bulk purchases, please contact Tyndale House Publishers at csresponse@tyndale.com, or call 1-855-277-9400.

Library of Congress Cataloging-in-Publication Data

A catalog record for this book is available from the Library of Congress.

ISBN 978-1-4964-4896-5

Printed in the United States of America

28 27 26 25 24 23 22
7 6 5 4 3 2 1

CONTENTS

A NOTE FROM THE AUTHOR

I have been in vocational ministry for more than four decades; and though I could fill several books with the sheer delights of such a role, *nothing* has brought me more joy over the years than seeing believers embrace the seven statements we will explore during this study. When people finally grasp who they are in Christ and what their participation means to the church, *everything* changes. Life begins to make sense. Love seems more possible. Light begins to penetrate all that had previously been dark.

In Christ, our identity is secured.

Our purpose is clarified.

Our mission is confirmed.

Our hearts start longing to cooperate with God.

Our lives become framed by seven simple "I am" statements that make all the difference.

During this study, you will be invited to grow in your understanding of the following key characteristics that mark the life of every Christian:

- I am a believer.
- I am a church member.
- I am a disciple.
- I am a servant.

- I am a witness.
- I am a prayer warrior.
- I am a Christian.

These days there is no shortage of groups that seek to define our identity. Democrat or Republican? On Facebook or Instagram? Using an Android or an iPhone? Where I'm from, the question was always about football: "Auburn or 'Bama?" But though these designations, and a thousand others, have their place, God longs for us to define ourselves by one fact, and one fact alone. He longs for us to find our identity *in Christ*—that is, to believe in his Son, know his Son, love his Son, and make it our life's work to be transformed into his Son's perfect image.

Christian should be the primary identity that people associate with us when they survey our lives. This study includes eight sessions—one introductory meeting and seven sessions focused on seven key statements—looking carefully at what it means to say, "I am a Christian." In the process, we'll answer questions such as these:

What thoughts do Christians think?
What actions do Christians take?
What priorities do Christians uphold?
What choices do Christians make?
What do Christians pray about?
Why do Christians serve?
How do Christians mature in their faith?
What brings Christians joy?

It's no exaggeration to say that I'm *ecstatic* for you as you begin the process of answering these and other vital questions about what it means to follow Jesus.

I Am a Christian Participant's Guide was created to help you deepen both your sense of intimacy with Jesus and your involvement with his bride, the church.

Each session includes both group-oriented discussion questions and opportunities for personal reflection. Your group leader will encourage you to share with the full group, but only those aspects of your story that you are comfortable sharing.

As you take this journey, I'm praying that curiosity will compel you, hope will inspire you, and ever-deepening intimacy with God will sustain you step-by-step.

OVERVIEW AND LEADER'S GUIDE

Planning Your Group Experience

This study was born of two driving beliefs: (1) As Christians, we ought to know what it *means* to be a Christian, and (2) we ought to understand why being connected to a local church is *essential* to realizing our full potential in Christ. There is no better way to set ourselves up for success in life as followers of Jesus than to impart these fundamental truths. Thus, I am deeply grateful for small group leaders like you.

Thank you—sincerely—for agreeing to lead an *I Am a Christian* group. I would offer you some sort of reward for your courage, but the real reward will be having a front-row seat to your group members' life-changing experiences. As they come to understand all that awaits them, as they deepen their connection to Jesus and his church, look out! There will be joy. There will be laughter. There will be amazement. There will be celebration of the undeniable goodness of God.

You will see people who have been sidelined for *years* get connected to the living, breathing body of Christ. You will see selfish people become excited about serving. You will see hard-hearted people learn to sacrifice on behalf of those in need.

The list could go on, but you get the idea. Great things are in store for your group—and for you as their leader.

You will want to be prepared for each session so you can steward this responsibility well. To that end, take some time to complete the following Foolproof Facilitation grid, making notes in the right-hand column of ideas you have or things you don't want to forget as you go.

FOOLPROOF FACILITATION

Tips for an Engaging Experience

☑	Consideration	Notes
❒	Choose your group. Ideally your group will number seven to ten members.	
❒	Obtain copies of *I Am a Christian* and this participant's guide for each group member.	
❒	Confirm all eight meeting dates before your first meeting. To cut down on preventable absences, be sure everyone knows ahead of time when the sessions—an introductory session plus seven study sessions—will occur. See "A Study in Eight Sessions" on page 4.	
❒	Familiarize yourself with the session sections noted below. Prior to your first meeting, preview this guide so that you know what's coming and when.	
❒	Obtain access (digital or hard copy) to the New Living Translation of the Bible. With one or two exceptions, every Scripture passage in this guide is drawn from the NLT.	
❒	Read and complete each lesson prior to the corresponding meeting. Be sure to carefully read the entire session's content before you gather for group time. Note the facilitation cues.	

❒	Preview each session's video prior to the meeting.	
❒	Pray, pray, and pray some more. We have a real enemy, and he would love nothing more than to distract us from spiritual growth. Prioritize praying for your group every day during this experience.	
❒	Communicate with group members. Ask how you can serve them, pray for them, encourage them, and support them.	
❒	Keep the group time moving along. Each session is based on a meeting time of 90 minutes (plus time for fellowship before and after the study). Allow time for people to participate, but keep an eye on the clock as you lead each session.	
❒	Draw out timid members and help subdue chatty ones. A variety of personalities make groups interesting, but you may need to create opportunities for quieter members to participate. Quiet doesn't mean uninvolved. It may just mean these members are thinking or don't want to interrupt.	
❒	Keep the group focused on the main thing. The twofold goals of this experience are (1) understanding what it means to be a Christian, and (2) understanding why participation in a local church is crucial to our lives as believers. When the discussion drifts from these goals, draw the group back to the primary focus.	
❒	Celebrate God's goodness and grace. One mark of a mature believer is giving God the glory, not seeking our own. Frequently remind your group of who is behind every positive step forward.	

In Matthew 18:20, Jesus says that "where two or three gather together as my followers, I am there among them." Rest assured that as you come together to study God's Word, to better understand his plan for the church, and to commit yourself to his will and ways, he is there, *with* you and *for* you, cheering you on.

A STUDY IN EIGHT SESSIONS

To maximize your group's discussion time, encourage group members to complete the entire content for each session prior to attending the corresponding group meeting.

Giving group members an opportunity to develop and "sit with" their answers to each session's questions before being asked to share their thoughts often helps them sort out what they truly think and discern what they're prepared to share with the full group.

Remember: Depending on their life experiences and current circumstances, some group members may not feel comfortable sharing some answers aloud. Though it's finc to invitc thcsc pcoplc to talk with you one-on-one outside of the group experience, always be respectful of requests for privacy, and never pressure someone to share with the group.

BUDGETING GROUP TIME

With the exception of the introductory session, which is an abbreviated meeting, each session in this study is designed to last 90 minutes, divided as follows:

- **Getting Started:** 10 minutes [Welcome/review/brief prayer]
- **Video and Reflection:** 15 minutes [Show the video and discuss the "Reflection on the Video" question.]

- **Group Discussion:** 55 minutes [You may not have time to discuss every question in each session, so be prepared to pick and choose the ones most relevant for your group.]
- **Taking It Home:** 10 minutes [Closing thoughts and group prayer]

Many groups prefer to enjoy a time of fellowship both before and after each session, which brings the total meeting time to around two hours. As group leader, be sure to communicate your time expectations to all group members prior to gathering for your first meeting.

SESSION 1

THE KICKOFF MEETING

Overview and Getting to Know Your Group

The first meeting will be an hour-long get-together to kick off the study with an icebreaker, an overview of the seven sessions, and a time of prayer. The group leader will hand out the book and participant's guide to each group member, screen the introductory session video, and answer any questions. During this introductory session, the group will address the following topics:

- Overview of the series and goals for the study
- Schedule for the remaining seven sessions
- Explanation about completing session content prior to each group meeting

Here is a suggested schedule for this initial meeting:

- ☐ Welcome to group members and opening prayer: 7 minutes
- ☐ Icebreaker: 10 minutes. Ask everyone to share something about themselves that nobody else (except maybe their spouse) would know.

- ☐ Overview of the remaining seven sessions: 10 minutes
- ☐ Introductory session video: 13 minutes
- ☐ Reflection on the video: 5 minutes. What does the phrase "I am a Christian" mean to you?
- ☐ Q&A: 10 minutes
- ☐ Closing prayer: 5 minutes

SESSION 2

I AM A BELIEVER

Knowing and Loving the Truth

We can't know who we are as Christians until we grasp who Jesus is.

[Recommended Reading]

Before you meet with your group to discuss session 2, read the introduction and chapter 1, "I Am a Believer," in *I Am a Christian.* Also read the session text and complete the exercises and questions below.

PREPARING YOUR HEART

[Complete the exercises in this section on your own before attending the group meeting. These are not for group discussion but to help you begin to connect to the topics that will be discussed in this session.]

Think of the ways you tend to *describe* yourself and *present* yourself to others. Maybe they're based on your position in your family—father or mother, son or daughter, brother or sister, aunt or uncle. Or perhaps you identify strongly with your occupation—teacher or programmer, grocery clerk or writer or painter, counselor or parole officer, pastor or mail carrier. Or maybe you define yourself by your other relationships—neighbor or friend, coworker or church member.

For all of us, what follows the phrase "I am . . ." matters greatly. Your identity sets the parameters for how you operate in the world, which is why it's important not to miss God's identity statement in Exodus 3:14.

1. Look up Exodus 3:14 and record the words here:

---

2. Why do you suppose God didn't elaborate on his identity here? What do you think this conveyed to his hearers?

---

3. Review the following characteristics that mark the life of every Christian. Which ones are the toughest for you to wrap your mind and heart around? Go ahead and check those boxes below.

- ☐ "I am a believer."
- ☐ "I am a church member."
- ☐ "I am a disciple."
- ☐ "I am a servant."
- ☐ "I am a witness."
- ☐ "I am a prayer warrior."
- ☐ "I am a Christian."

During this study, we will discuss what it means to clothe ourselves in these aspects of Christianity. As you work through each one, I encourage you to pay special attention to the specific aspects of your identity in Christ that are a challenge for you to embrace.

- Ask God to help you understand what it means to be a disciple, a servant, a witness, a prayer warrior—or whichever aspect of being a Christian you struggle with.
- Ask God to give you opportunities to shore up that area of discipleship.
- Ask God to give you victories in that area so you can build some momentum toward adopting that facet as a regular part of your lifestyle.

In the space below, jot a brief prayer to God regarding the help you hope he'll offer you in growing in the area you noted above.

GETTING STARTED

[After the group leader's opening remarks and review, pause for a brief prayer before watching the video.]

REFLECTION ON THE VIDEO

What does it mean to you to be a believer?

GROUP DISCUSSION

[Complete the exercises in this section prior to meeting for session 2, and be prepared to share some of your answers with your group.]

Let's turn our attention now to what it means to truly be "a believer" in Jesus Christ. What, exactly, do believers believe? What are the common truths to which they hold? And how do those beliefs affect their daily lives? In this session, we'll look at four beliefs that identify us as followers of Jesus and three key practices that mark the life of a believer.

What Do Christians Believe?

Though there are undeniable differences among Christians, the beliefs that unite us are stronger. In fact, there are at least four striking similarities that immediately identify believers in Christ. These similarities are core beliefs of the Christian faith:

- The Bible is the Word of God.
- There is only one God, and he is triune—Father, Son, and Spirit.
- Every person is created in God's image.
- Every person needs salvation from sin.

Let's take each belief in turn.

Belief #1: The Bible Is the Word of God

What we call "the Bible" or "the Holy Bible" today took more than 1,500 years to write—from about 1400 BC to about AD 90. Written by more than forty people—fishermen, tentmakers, doctors, and priests alike—it contains sixty-six books and covers everything from the creation of the world to what heaven will be like for us someday.

According to its own testimony, though the Bible was written by human writers, it was authored by God himself. Fill in the details of what 2 Timothy 3:16-17 says about this process:

All ______________ is ______________ by
______________ and is useful to ______________
us what is ______________ and to make us realize
what is ______________ in our ______________. It
______________ us when we are ______________
and teaches us to do what is ______________. God
uses it to ______________ and ______________ his
people to do every good ______________.

1. If you were to put into words how you view the Bible today, what words would you use? Select a few from the list below or come up with entries of your own.

- ☐ Inerrant
- ☐ Questionable
- ☐ Suspicious
- ☐ Convicting
- ☐ Infallible
- ☐ Complex
- ☐ Reliable
- ☐ Curious
- ☐ Contradictory
- ☐ Instructive
- ☐ Understandable
- ☐ Coherent
- ☐ Straightforward
- ☐ Unreliable
- ☐ Unified
- ☐ Meaningful
- ☐ Intrusive
- ☐ Frustrating
- ☐ Inspiring
- ☐ Enlightening
- ☐ Confusing
- ☐ Debatable
- ☐ Holy
- ☐ Unifying
- ☐ Wise
- ☐ Destructive
- ☐ Thoughtful
- ☐ Helpful
- ☐ Sharp
- ☐ Incomplete

2. How did you come to your current perception of God's Word? What assumptions or firsthand experiences have shaped your views here?

If we begin to doubt the truth of any portion of Scripture, we undermine our confidence that any other part is true as well.

---

3. What hope do the words of Hebrews 4:12 (see sidebar) give you for growing in your understanding of God's Word over time?

Belief #2: There Is Only One God, and He Is Triune—Father, Son, and Spirit

The second belief that Christians share is that there is only one God, and that he exists in three persons.

This is also known as the doctrine of the Trinity.

After Jesus was raised from the dead and was due to return to his Father's side in heaven, he asked his followers to continue his work here on earth. His words to them are commonly known as the Great Commission:

> I have been given all authority in heaven and on earth. Therefore, go and make disciples of all the nations, baptizing them in the name of the Father and the Son and the Holy Spirit. Teach these new disciples to obey all the commands I have given you. And be sure of this: I am with you always, even to the end of the age.
> MATTHEW 28:18-20

The word of God is alive and powerful. It is sharper than the sharpest two-edged sword, cutting between soul and spirit, between joint and marrow. It exposes our innermost thoughts and desires. (Hebrews 4:12)

Everyone who is a true believer has encountered all three persons of the Trinity. It is the Holy

Spirit who alerts us to our need for salvation; it is God's Son, Jesus, who sacrificed his very life so that our sins could be atoned for; and it is God the Father who welcomes us into his eternal presence, now seeing us not in our sinful state but through Christ's blood, which was shed for us.

Look up the following verses, noting how each one supports the ideas from the previous paragraph. Place a check mark beside the entry that most resonates with you today, and then explain to your group why you selected the one you did.

☑	VERSES	NOTES
❒	John 3:16	
❒	John 6:44	
❒	John 14:21	
❒	John 16:7-8	
❒	Acts 1:8	
❒	Romans 5:8	

Belief #3: Every Person Is Created in God's Image

In Genesis 1:26-27, we read these words from God:

> "Let us make human beings in our image, to be like us. They will reign over the fish in the sea, the birds in the sky, the livestock, all the wild animals on the earth, and the small animals that scurry along the ground."
>
> So God created human beings in his own image.
> In the image of God he created them;
> male and female he created them.

4. Based on the previous discussion, why do you suppose Genesis 1:26 uses the personal pronouns it does when it says, "Let *us* make human beings in *our* image, to be like *us*" (italics added)?

5. What do you think it means to be created in God's image?

6. How do you think relational conflicts might be more quickly resolved if both parties truly believed that the other person was created in the image of God? What dynamics or attitudes might change?

Belief #4: Every Person Needs Salvation from Sin

Yes, it's true that you and I and every other human being have been created in the image of almighty God. Know what else is true? We have *terribly* marred that image. By our selfishness, sin, and rebellion, we have made the image of God in us nearly indistinguishable. That's why this fourth belief exists: Because of our sinfulness, we need salvation through Jesus Christ.

> If you openly declare that Jesus is Lord and believe in your heart that God raised him from the dead, you will be saved. For it is by believing in your heart that you are made right with God, and it is by openly declaring your faith that you are saved. As the Scriptures tell us, "Anyone who trusts in him will never be disgraced." (Romans 10:9-11)

7. Record below what you learn about salvation from Romans 10:9-11 (see sidebar).
If you ____________________
you will ____________________.
For it is by ____________________
that you are ____________________,
and it is by ____________________
that you are ____________________.

8. How do these straightforward steps align with your experience of surrendering your life to Jesus? Discuss with your group the similarities and differences you see.

____

____

What Do Believers Do?

It's one thing to say that we're "believers," but Scripture is clear that unless our actions back up that claim—matching our walk to our talk—then we aren't to be trusted. Look up James 2:14-17 and answer the following questions:

9. If Scripture is clear that we are saved by grace and not by works (see Ephesians 2:8-10), what does James mean when he asks, "Can that kind of faith"—that is, the kind of faith that isn't accompanied by actions—"save anyone?"

____

____

10. What practical example does James offer to make his point?

____

____

11. Can you relate? When have you wished someone well without actually helping him or her in a time of real need? What constraint kept you from doing more?

- ☐ Lack of time
- ☐ Lack of money
- ☐ Lack of energy
- ☐ Lack of bandwidth to care about someone else's problems
- ☐ Something else: ______________________

12. Let's pause here for a moment and check in. What thoughts are occurring to you as you consider the idea that faith requires *works* if it is to be considered genuine faith?

____

____

+ + +

We have said that faith without works is useless or dead. As the apostle Paul says in Galatians 5:22-23, genuine faith will produce the fruit of the Spirit in us. As we surrender more and more of ourselves to the Holy Spirit, spiritual fruit will naturally show itself in our lives. The question that may be on your mind now is, *Well, then, how do I give the Spirit more room to live and move?*

It's a great question.

Fortunately, it's one that God has answered for us in Scripture.

There are straightforward practices—often called *spiritual disciplines*—that you and I can implement that will automatically help us surrender more of our lives to God. In this next section, let's look at three such practices that will help us *activate* our faith day by day. They are as follows:

- Reading and living according to God's Word, the Bible
- Frequent and regular prayer
- Telling people who don't know Jesus about the gift of grace

Let's consider each in turn.

Believers Read and Live according to God's Word

We have already looked in this session at the importance of believing that the Bible is the Word of God. Now let's build on that understanding by adding another piece to the puzzle: Believers not only believe that the Bible is God's Word; they also *read* the Bible and *live according to what it says.*

13. Do you make a practice of reading Scripture on a regular basis? Describe to your group what that looks like in your daily life.

14. Which of the following benefits would you hope to realize by prioritizing daily Bible reading?

- ☐ Know God better
- ☐ Become wiser
- ☐ Experience greater peace in life
- ☐ Grow in your faith
- ☐ Realize your need for God
- ☐ Receive forgiveness
- ☐ Encounter truth
- ☐ Be filled with hope
- ☐ Increase in faith
- ☐ Be protected from false teaching
- ☐ Find instruction on how to live
- ☐ Seize opportunities to worship God
- ☐ Something else: ____________________

15. Take a look at Matthew 4:4. What do you think would be true of you if you lived not by physical bread alone but by spiritual sustenance, by "every word that comes from the mouth of God"? Jot down ideas that come to mind:

____

____

Believers Pray Frequently and Regularly

To make more room for the Holy Spirit in their lives, believers read and live according to God's Word. And here's something else: *They pray*. They pray often. They pray easily. They pray fervently. They pray from a place of joy. As I noted in *I Am a Christian*, "prayer might be the most talked about but least acted upon spiritual discipline of the Christian faith." Because we will devote an entire session to the subject of prayer later in the book, here I'd like you to simply respond to my assertion about prayer by answering the two questions below.

16. What do you think of the claim that "prayer might be the most talked about but least acted upon spiritual discipline of the Christian faith"?

17. Why do think there is such a disconnect between what we as believers *say* and what we *do* regarding prayer?

Prayer is not merely a discipline; it is an honor of the highest magnitude.

Believers Eagerly Spread the Good News

Believers read and live according to the Word of God. They pray frequently and fervently. And they *eagerly spread the good news of the gospel*, knowing that this is Jesus' mandate to all his followers.

18. When was the last time you shared the gospel with someone? What opportunities might you use to connect with nonbelievers in a genuine, loving way?

TAKING IT HOME

Before you close your group session, take a few minutes to pray. Ask God to help you with any or all of the following steps of spiritual growth, in addition to others that come to your group members' minds:

- ☐ To better understand our identity as believers
- ☐ To more faithfully practice the spiritual disciplines of reading the Bible, living according to Scripture, praying, and telling others about the good news of grace

Next, to confirm what you've learned in this session, note in the space below one action you plan to take—between now and session 3—to make progress on your spiritual journey.

SESSION 3

I AM A CHURCH MEMBER

Being Part of a Forever Family

The New Testament does not have a plan for growing us as Christians outside of the local church.

[Recommended Reading]

Before you meet with your group to discuss session 3, read chapter 2, "I Am a Church Member," in *I Am a Christian.* Also read the session text and complete the exercises and questions below.

PREPARING YOUR HEART

[Complete the exercises in this section on your own before attending the group meeting. These are not for group discussion but to help you begin to connect to the topics that will be discussed in this session.]

It is one of the more curious aspects of the human experience. When you and I were born, we were dropped into families not of our choosing. We arrived on the scene and were handed to an adult who now was tasked with caring for our every need. I think you'd agree that that was a pretty vulnerable position to find ourselves in! And yet we learn from King David that God intentionally places people in families (Psalm 68:6).

There was a man named Nicodemus, a Jewish religious leader who was a Pharisee. After dark one evening, he came to speak with Jesus. "Rabbi," he said, "we all know that God has sent you to teach us. Your miraculous signs are evidence that God is with you."

Jesus replied, "I tell you the truth, unless you are born again, you cannot see the Kingdom of God."

"What do you mean?" exclaimed Nicodemus. "How can an old man go back into his mother's womb and be born again?"

Jesus replied, "I assure you, no one can enter the Kingdom of God without being born of water and the Spirit. Humans can reproduce only human life, but the Holy Spirit gives birth to spiritual life. So don't be surprised when I say, 'You must be born again.' The wind blows wherever it wants. Just as you can hear the wind but can't tell where it comes from or where it is going, so you can't explain how people are born of the Spirit." (John 3:1-8)

Just as God intentionally places people in earthly families, he also places each of us in a *spiritual* family upon our "second birth." Read John 3:1-8 in the sidebar and then answer the questions that follow.

1. We looked previously at the idea that it is the Holy Spirit who draws people to God. This second birth, then, is a Spirit-generated birth, a *spiritual* birth. What was it about our first birth (the birth from our mother's womb) that points to our needing a second birth (the birth from the Holy Spirit)?

2. What words would you use to describe your second—or spiritual—birth?

Our earthly families were intended both to care for our needs and to receive care from us as we grew in our ability to help meet their needs, and our spiritual family is intended to work in the same way.

GETTING STARTED

[After the group leader's opening remarks and review, pause for a brief prayer before watching the video.]

REFLECTION ON THE VIDEO

What does it mean to be a committed member of a church?

GROUP DISCUSSION

[Complete the exercises in this section prior to meeting for session 3, and be prepared to share some of your answers with your group.]

Our spiritual family—the universal church—is intended to run like a well-functioning family. A singular "body," as the apostle Paul called it, *completely unified*, even as it is composed of many parts.

1. Read 1 Corinthians 12:12-31. Based on the concept that each of us is part of one body—one central family unit—in Christ, capture your thoughts on the topics below.

   Diversity in the body of Christ:

   Unity in the body:

   Necessity of each of the body's parts:

   Harmony within the body:

2. With the apostle Paul's words from 1 Corinthians 12 fresh in your mind, describe for your group a time when you saw Christ's body—the church—working as a unified whole . . . as a *family*.

- What were the circumstances involved?

- Were you part of the family at the time or observing from outside?

- What dynamics did you see unfold?

- What was the ultimate effect of the unity you experienced or observed?

We get the term *member* from the Bible's discussion of the church, not from the secular world of civic organizations or country clubs. A member, or part, is what is necessary to make the body whole.

Take a minute to collect your thoughts by jotting down the memory in the space below. Then share it with your group.

+ + +

It's tempting to believe that occasions such as the one you described in response to the previous question are rarities, that seeing the church work as it is supposed to is about as likely as spotting a unicorn in the wild. This simply isn't the case. As with so many spiritual topics, we have a tendency to complicate things that God made plain. Church membership is one such topic, and yet a careful review of Scripture, along with our own empirical evidence, reminds us that plugging into the family that God has placed us in as his spiritual sons and daughters is one of the simplest, most natural things we can do.

As we look at five key practices of plugged-in family members, it is worth noting that in Acts 2:42-47, the people came together in community *immediately after* they came to faith in Jesus Christ. Just after Peter preached the gospel and called people to repentance, "those who believed what Peter said were baptized and added to the church that day—about 3,000 in all" (Acts 2:41).

- They believed.
- They were baptized.
- They were added to the church.

I love this progression for its straightforward simplicity. Believe. Be baptized. Join the life of God's family.

Now, on to those practices I mentioned. What determines whether you are a plugged-in family member, an active participant in Jesus' church? I'll give you all five here, and then we'll look at each in turn:

- Church members gather.
- Church members serve.
- Church members give.
- Church members unify.
- Church members pray.

Church Members Gather

One of the clearest mandates in all of Scripture has to do with our first key practice, which is that Church members *gather*. Fill in the blanks below with what you learn from Hebrews 10:23-25:

> Let us hold ________________ without ________________ to the hope we affirm, for God can be ________________ to keep his ________________. Let us think of ways to ________________ one another to acts of ________________ and good ________________. And let us not ________________ our meeting ________________, as some people do, but ________________ one another, especially now that the ________________ of his ________________ is drawing ________________.

3. Thinking back on your own experience, when you've chosen to go to church or to plug in to the life of a church for a given period of time, why have you generally done so?

- ☐ To serve
- ☐ To be served
- ☐ To be encouraged
- ☐ To encourage others
- ☐ To let my priorities be known
- ☐ To feel included
- ☐ To comply with a loved one's wishes
- ☐ To be available to help people in need
- ☐ To worship God
- ☐ To detox from a busy week
- ☐ To obey the Bible's command
- ☐ To set a good example
- ☐ To encourage my pastor
- ☐ To assuage my guilt
- ☐ To remind myself what matters
- ☐ Because I love my church

One of the clearest commitments of a healthy marriage—and also a healthy church—is simply showing up.

4. Based on the exhortations in this passage, what are the two primary purposes for gathering frequently as the church, the body of Christ?

- To motivate one another to acts of ______________ and good ______________
- To ______________________ one another

How well do your experiences with the church reflect these two primary purposes? Which of the following statements do you resonate with? Offer your group members a little context regarding why you are answering the way you are.

- ☐ "I've honestly never seen the church operate this way. I wish I had, but I haven't."
- ☐ "I can think of a few specific occasions when I saw the church operate in this loving, encouraging, service-oriented way, and it has been awe-inspiring every time."
- ☐ "I know the church is far from perfect—it's made up of far-from-perfect people, after all. Still, I'd say that generally speaking, this is how I'm used to seeing the church operate. I *often* see people motivating others to love and good works. I *often* see people encouraging one another. I can think of many times when members of the church have shown up for each other in these ways. It's a wonderful and life-giving thing."

+ + +

Regardless of how you responded to the previous question, it's important to remember that before any of the laudable events of Acts 2 could occur—the worshiping, the learning, the generosity, the prayer—the people of God had to gather.

Church Members Serve

Perhaps the greatest set of verses on the type of servanthood you and I are to emulate as followers of Jesus shows up in a letter from the apostle Paul to the church at Philippi.

You must have the same attitude that Christ Jesus had. Though he was God, he did not think of equality with God as something to cling to. Instead, he gave up his divine privileges; he took the humble position of a slave and was born as a human being. When he appeared in human form, he humbled himself in obedience to God and died a criminal's death on a cross. Therefore, God elevated him to the place of highest honor and gave him the name above all other names, that at the name of Jesus every knee should bow, in heaven and on earth and under the earth, and every tongue declare that Jesus Christ is Lord, to the glory of God the Father.

PHILIPPIANS 2:5-11

5. Based on this passage, record what you notice about Jesus' attitude, his actions, and the acknowledgment (or commendation) from God he received.

Jesus' attitude:

Jesus' actions:

The Father's acknowledgment:

6. If you were to distill what you learned from Philippians 2:5-11, what are two or three character traits you would like to grow in? Share one of your answers with your group.

7. In the space below, describe a time when you served in the context of the church. What ministry were you serving with? What situations did you face? How was the experience for you?

8. How would the character traits you identified above have helped you to thrive in that serving capacity?

Your role as a church member is to *serve*, not to be served. It is to minister, not to be ministered to. Serve. Serve again. Serve with joy.

9. Based on your group's discussion, what do you suppose is the real reason God asks us to serve him by serving his church?

Church Members Give

If you want to stir up a fiery debate, simply ask people what they think about money and the church, and how it seems the church is always asking for money. Oh, the sparks will fly!

10. Go ahead and have at it for a few minutes: What do you and your fellow group members think of when you hear the combination "money and church"?

It seems that most of the debate regarding financial giving in the church is focused on what we are *required* to give rather than on what we are *blessed* to give. As I mentioned in *I Am a Christian*, "one of the most financially liberating moments for me was when I finally understood that I have the joyous opportunity to give freely and generously rather than focusing on giving at a certain level. . . . Giving to God's mission and his church is a gift and an opportunity—not something to be neglected."

Which word better frames how you view giving to the Church today: *obligation* or *blessing*? Why? Jot down some of the differences between the two below.

MY THOUGHTS ON GIVING	
Obligation	**Blessing**

11. In 2 Corinthians 9:7-8 (see sidebar), what three promises does the apostle Paul make on God's behalf to the person who holds a celebratory posture toward financial giving in the church?

12. Before Paul lays out the promises, he confirms how God feels about cheerful givers. What does he say?

13. If you were to experience an unexpected deepening in your sense of cheerfulness toward giving, what pressing needs in the world would you want to help meet first? Why?

+ + +

Before moving on, consider taking a few minutes to ask God to open doors of opportunity in one or more of the specific areas of need you noted. What might God do in and through you?

Heavenly Father, . . .

You must each decide in your heart how much to give. And don't give reluctantly or in response to pressure. "For God loves a person who gives cheerfully." And God will generously provide all you need. Then you will always have everything you need and plenty left over to share with others. (2 Corinthians 9:7-8)

Church Members Unify

If you've been part of a local church for any length of time—and especially if you're a regular giver—then you know how easy it is to start believing that the church is there to meet your needs, honor your preferences, and consider your opinions. I don't think that church members *intend* to act like spoiled brats; it's just a temptation that seems to overtake most people I know—myself included.

Indeed, of the hundreds upon hundreds of church disputes that my team at Church Answers and I have mediated, surprisingly few have been about the important stuff, such as doctrine, eldership, or discipleship. What *do* they typically center on? The feeling that the pastor preaches too long. Or that the sanctuary is kept at too warm a temperature. Or that the drummer in the worship band is too loud.

Can you relate?

14. When have you felt a little irked over something at church that you're willing to admit wasn't weighty in nature? Note a few ideas below and divulge one or two to your group.

It's tough to live at peace with people who don't think the way we think, act the way we act, or share our sense of propriety. And yet that's exactly what God has asked us as his sons and daughters to do: to do all we can to "live in peace with everyone" (Romans 12:18).

In case you think such a mandate is impossible, let me draw your attention back to the early church. Read Acts 4:32 in the sidebar, and answer with your group the questions that follow.

15. Based on the description of the early church in Acts 4:32, what actions and attitudes foster unity in a church?

All the believers were united in heart and mind. And they felt that what they owned was not their own, so they shared everything they had. (Acts 4:32)

16. What fears or frustrations would you have to let go of to be a true unifier at your church?

17. If you were known as a unifier in the church, what evidence do you hope people would point to regarding your attitude, your words, and your actions?

Church Members Pray

Church members are careful to gather. They are eager to serve. They are faithful to give. They can be counted on to unify. And then there's this, the fifth and final practice: *They pray.* Consistently and fervently. Soon we will spend an entire session on the subject of prayer, but here I'd like to focus our attention on the kinds of prayers that faithful church members pray.

Several months ago on the Church Answers website, I posted seven specific prayers that all believers can pray for their pastors and local churches. Using the prompts below, take a few minutes as a group to pray for your own pastor and church.

For the Church

- *Pray for protection in spiritual warfare.* The enemy seeks to destroy the witness of churches by attacking the people within them—especially pastors. Pray that God by his Spirit would protect everyone in your church.

- *Pray for families.* Families are under attack today in ways never seen in our culture. Pray for marriages to be strengthened. Pray for parents to lead their children well. Pray for unity in all situations. Pray for prodigals to return home.

- *Pray for spiritual growth.* Ask God to help each person in your church experience spiritual growth today. Whatever their next step is, pray that God, by his Spirit, would embolden them to take it.

- *Pray for leadership.* Pray that current leaders will serve wisely and humbly and that new leaders would be raised up to meet the demands of your church as it thrives.

For Your Pastor

- *Pray for protection from critics and naysayers.* Being teachable is far different from being willing to be torn down. Standing up to preach week after week is challenging. Pray that your pastor would be shielded from harmful comments (or helpful comments delivered in harmful ways).

- *Pray for the preaching ministry overall.* Ask God to give the preachers and teachers at your church self-discipline and divine insight as they prepare messages to deliver to the congregation. If your church doesn't also have people praying for the person teaching *while that teaching is happening*, consider starting such a ministry. All it takes is two or three faithful pray-ers gathered in a quiet room during the service.

- *Pray for rest.* Sometimes it seems as if we expect our pastors to be mini versions of God: omnipotent, omniscient, and omnipresent. Of course, no pastor can pull this off. Pray that your pastor would have time to rest this week (and every week) and would truly be able to rest.

TAKING IT HOME

Think of new ways you could commit to each of the five practices we mentioned in this session. I've offered some prompts to get you going, but feel free to add your own thoughts.

The opt-out excuse I will ditch this week so that I can be a church member who *gathers* is . . .

The action I will take to *serve* someone in the church this week is . . .

The purchase I will forgo so that I can *give* financially to the church this week is . . .

The issue I will let go of in order to *unify* my church and live at peace with everyone is . . .

The time each day that I will *pray* for my church and my pastor this week is . . .

SESSION 4

I AM A DISCIPLE

Following Only Jesus

Until we get to heaven, we are supposed to grow as Christians. . . . We are commanded to continue growing as fully devoted followers of Christ.

[Recommended Reading]

Before you meet with your group to discuss session 4, read chapter 3, "I Am a Disciple," in *I Am a Christian*. Also read the session text and complete the exercises and questions below.

PREPARING YOUR HEART

[Complete the exercises in this section on your own before attending the group meeting. These are not for group discussion but to help you begin to connect to the topics that will be discussed in this session.]

In sessions 2 and 3, we looked at the first two "I am" statements for Christians: *I am a believer* and *I am a church member*. Each of those statements reflects a specific point in time—the moment when we surrender our lives to Jesus and begin going God's way instead of our own; the moment when we link arms with our fellow believers and say, "I'm in."

This fourth session turns to a statement that reflects not a specific point in time but a general direction in our lives. The statement is this: *I am a disciple.*

If you were to look up the derivation of the word *disciple* as it is used in the New Testament—such as in John 8:31—you would discover that it means a *learner*, an *imitator*, a *follower* of another.

A *disciple* is a learner, an imitator, a follower of a teacher, an adherent of another's thoughts and actions.

Based on this definition, if you were to scrutinize your current thought patterns, attitudes, habits, compulsions, and routines—both online and in daily life—who or what would you say you're a "disciple" of these days? Whose voices are loudest in your life lately? What are you giving your time and energy to? Where are you turning for comfort? Who are you following? Who are you listening to?

Well, how did you do? Did Jesus make your list? By the end of this session, I hope he will top *every* list.

GETTING STARTED

[After the group leader's opening remarks and review, pause for a brief prayer before watching the video.]

REFLECTION ON THE VIDEO

What does it mean to be a disciple of Jesus?

GROUP DISCUSSION

[Complete the exercises in this section prior to meeting for session 4, and be prepared to share some of your answers with your group.]

In Matthew 28:18-20 (see sidebar), when Jesus issued what we call the Great Commission, he gave his followers explicit instructions about what to do after he returned to heaven from earth. Read the passage and answer the questions that follow.

1. What three things did Jesus tell his followers to do?

2. What knowledge or skills do we need in order to accomplish discipleship as Jesus defines it, which centers on teaching new believers about their identity in Christ (the confession of faith that is made public in

Jesus came and told his disciples, "I have been given all authority in heaven and on earth. Therefore, go and make disciples of all the nations, baptizing them in the name of the Father and the Son and the Holy Spirit. Teach these new disciples to obey all the commands I have given you. And be sure of this: I am with you always, even to the end of the age." (Matthew 28:18-20)

baptism) and the lifestyle of obedience to all his commands? Capture your thoughts in the space below and then share your ideas with your group.

Discipleship is a multidirectional reality—we must be discipled ourselves in order to disciple others. Indeed, the moment we forget that we are learners as well as teachers is the moment we become ineffective at both. Spend a few minutes reflecting on your attention to these two areas of spiritual growth.

3. In what ways are you pursuing spiritual growth? Think of your attention to Bible reading and teaching as well as the relationships you are investing in. Are there commitments you need to make to give more attention to being discipled?

4. In what ways are you discipling others? What relationships are you pursuing with the goal of helping others draw closer to Christ? Are there commitments you need to make to give more attention to making disciples?

+ + +

"Being discipled" is all about growing in Christlikeness. Look up and read the following verses, noting in the right-hand column what we experience as we are discipled by Jesus.

EFFECTS OF DISCIPLESHIP	
Verse(s)	**By-product/Blessing of Christ's Transforming Work in Our Lives**
Romans 12:1-2	
Acts 3:19	
2 Corinthians 5:17	
Ephesians 4:30-32	
2 Thessalonians 3:5	

Because you and I are "in Christ," we are destined for completeness in him and the blessing of all the things these verses describe. But so often both our effort and our experience fall short. If you've ever stumbled over the words in Matthew 5:48 that tell us to "be perfect, even as your Father in heaven is perfect," and you've wondered how on earth we're supposed to become *perfect* when we are undeniably imperfect people living in an undeniably imperfect world, then this word is for you: It is *by God's power*—that's how.

5. In what areas of the Christian life do you find yourself relying on yourself and your own power rather than God's power? How could you change that dynamic?

6. What might change in your life if you relied more on God's power to change you and less on your own power to change yourself?

Discipleship is a cooperative process between us and God. We don't just sit back and expect God to produce fruit in us. But neither can we bear any fruit apart from Christ. As Paul told the Philippian believers, "Work hard to show the results of your salvation, obeying God with deep reverence and fear." But in the same breath, he also said, "God is working in you, giving you the desire and power to do what pleases him" (Philippians 2:12-13). In other words, it is true that God is the only one who can make us grow in him *and* we will only grow in him if we are obeying his commands. It's a paradox we see borne out in Scripture and in our own lives.

7. Looking back on your spiritual growth, what were the circumstances surrounding times of great spiritual growth? What experiences did God bring into your life that were a catalyst to growth? What did you do during those times in your life to become a better disciple?

8. Take a look at the wording of 2 Corinthians 3:17-18 in *The Message* version (see the sidebar). What words and phrases are used to describe the process of discipleship—our becoming more and more like Jesus? What words or phrases might you use to describe your own experience of discipleship?

Sometimes believers, especially those new to faith in Jesus Christ, are tempted to be skeptical when they hear about how, over time, they will become more and more like Jesus as they continue surrendering their will to the will of their heavenly Father, about how they will be better . . .

and kinder . . .

and gentler . . .

and wiser . . .

and more patient . . .

and more joyful . . .

and more self-controlled . . .

. . . and they *just can't see it.*

They don't believe these things will ever be true for them. Why? Because they know what they're capable of! They know their own thoughts. They know the words they're liable to say. They know the actions they're capable of

When God is personally present, a living Spirit, that old, constricting legislation is recognized as obsolete. We're free of it! All of us! Nothing between us and God, our faces shining with the brightness of his face. And so we are transfigured much like the Messiah, our lives gradually becoming brighter and more beautiful as God enters our lives and we become like him. (2 Corinthians 3:17-18, MSG)

taking. And so they think, *Perfect? I'm all for a miracle, but even with God's power it's probably not going to happen for me.*

Can you relate to this type of thinking?

9. Describe a time when you have sabotaged your own growth, believing that you were somehow excluded from God's promise to change his children for the better as we walk with him.

Your Growth Thus Far

The fact is, you and I have been growing steadily in Jesus since the day we first said *yes* to him. Want proof? Let's take a look.

10. On the grid below, take a few minutes to record (or review) some of the growth spurts you've seen during the time you've been following Jesus. (If you're a brand-new believer, you might be logging progress over days, whereas longtime followers of Jesus might be logging progress over years.)

Jot down a general topic on the left side. In the right-hand column, expand on what that growth has looked like in your life. An example has been provided to get you thinking in this direction.

SPIRITUAL GROWTH I'VE KNOWN

Topic	**Effects of This Growth**
Example: Self-control	Used to lose my cool with the kids and have to apologize for the same stuff day after day. The trend has definitely shifted. I still feel irritated sometimes, but I'm far less likely to react poorly now. I actually *want* to be tender with them.

Though the growth we have experienced may have been punctuated with spiritual setbacks, and though our overall growth trajectory may resemble less of a straight up-and-to-the-right line and more of an erratic set of ups and downs, *we've grown*. God's transformative power has been active in our lives.

We've grown, and we'll continue to grow. That brings us to the next step in this exercise.

The Growth You Seek

If you were to lay out the kind of growth you'd like to see going forward in your life, what examples would you cite? The apostle Paul, writing to the church at Corinth, exhorts us as believers to "examine [ourselves] to see whether [our] faith is genuine" (2 Corinthians 13:5).

11. Upon such an examination, which aspects of your character need an extra dose of God's divinely transformative ways?

Do you want to be more forgiving of those who wrong you?

Do you want to be more patient with members of your immediate family?

Do you want to be open to deeper connections with fellow believers instead of always prioritizing other things?

Do you want to pray reflexively when crisis strikes?

Do you want to gain wisdom that will help you make good choices and offer wise advice to others?

Do you want to offer a helping hand to someone instead of keeping to yourself?

Describe the ways you want to change or the person you long to become:

Maybe you know exactly the areas you'd like to see God help you with. Maybe those areas are a bit unclear. Either way, ask God for confirmation of where he's at work in your life . . . and for courage to join him in that work.

Note your prayer in the space below.

Heavenly Father, . . .

Your Present Growth Advantage

12. Which theme rose to the surface as you asked God for insight in the previous section? Did several of your desired areas of growth revolve around money? relationships? letting go of habits that aren't edifying for you? Log that theme in the box below.

You must not be content to merely have the title of *Christian*. You must seek to be a better Christian every day.

Let me remind you of the mind-blowing truth we touched on earlier. "God is working in you," Paul says, "giving you the desire and the power to do what pleases him" (Philippians 2:13).

Did you catch that? Log it here:

God not only gives us the power to change but also the ______________________ to do so!

Our loving heavenly Father changes our desires so we want what honors him.

13. What do you think of the above statement? How have you seen God change your desires as you submit to his work in your life? Share your thoughts with your group.

____

____

✚ ✚ ✚

TAKING IT HOME

If you're game for a closing challenge between now and your next meeting, return to the Preparing Your Heart section of this session on page 42. Select one of the entries from your list of current influencers that is not serving you well and replace that influencer with the Lord Jesus this week. Give to God the time and attention you normally give to that influence—by reading your Bible, praying, or spending time worshiping God through song.

SESSION 5

I AM A SERVANT

Freely Choosing to Be Last

Being a servant is not just choosing to be last;
it is desiring to be last.

[Recommended Reading]

Before you meet with your group to discuss session 5, read chapter 4, "I Am a Servant," in *I Am a Christian*. Also read the session text and complete the exercises and questions below.

PREPARING YOUR HEART

[Complete the exercises in this section on your own before attending the group meeting. These are not for group discussion but to help you begin to connect to the topics that will be discussed in this session.]

This session is about what you and I treasure. It's about our treasures here on earth—how we get them, what we think of them—and also our treasures in heaven. It's about what Jesus says concerning which location should hold more of our treasure. And it's about what must be put to rest in our fleshly human natures to uphold the values that Jesus says his followers must uphold.

The mandate is crystal clear and is probably one you're familiar with. Fill in the blanks below with the words of Matthew 20:26-28:

Whoever wants to be a ________________ among you must be your ________________, and whoever wants to be ________________ among you must become your ________________. For even the ________________ of Man came not to be ________________ but to ________________ ________________ and to ________________ his ________________ as a ________________ for many.

1. From firsthand experience, what behaviors do you tend to see in people who are looking not to serve but to be served?

2. On the flip side, what behaviors do you tend to see in people who believe their purpose is to serve others?

3. Based on the perspective of those who know you best, which type of person are you?

- ☐ Friends and family members would say I'm generally the one serving.
- ☐ Friends and family members would say I'm happy to let others pick up the slack.

4. What do you think keeps those who don't serve from serving more? Check any options from the lineup below that resonate with you, or add your own to the mix. Then share your thoughts with the group.

- ☐ They don't want to be seen as weak.
- ☐ They have enough to manage in their own lives without taking on the burdens of others.
- ☐ They feel entitled to a little TLC.
- ☐ They don't even realize they're not pulling their weight.
- ☐ Something else: ____________________

GETTING STARTED

[After the group leader's opening remarks and review, pause for a brief prayer before watching the video.]

REFLECTION ON THE VIDEO

What does it mean for you to be a servant?

GROUP DISCUSSION

[Complete the exercises in this section prior to meeting for session 5, and be prepared to share some of your answers with your group.]

To open your discussion, invite each group member to respond to this assertion:

Being a servant is not just choosing to be last;
it is desiring to be last.

In the New Testament, one of Jesus' key themes is the idea of laying down our own preferences for the sake of others. We looked earlier at Paul's words in Philippians 2:5-11 regarding assuming the posture of Jesus, who came to earth in humility to die for our sins. The setup to that passage says this:

> Don't be selfish; don't try to impress others. Be humble, thinking of others as better than yourselves. Don't look out only for your own interests, but take an interest in others, too.
> PHILIPPIANS 2:3-4

1. There's a lot to those two brief verses, isn't there? As you read the passage, which of the following exhortations caught your attention? Which one gave you the feeling that a growth opportunity might be in your future?

☐ Don't be selfish.
☐ Don't try to impress others.
☐ Be humble.
☐ Think of others as better than yourself.
☐ Don't look out only for your own interests.
☐ Take an interest in others, too.

In Acts 20:35, Luke records the words of Jesus, who said, "It is more blessed to give than to receive."

2. When have you found this truism to be . . . well, *true*? Describe the situation to the group, explaining how the fulfillment you gained by giving exceeded any benefit you could have realized by keeping your resources for yourself.

The beauty of living a life devoted to God is that in doing so, we are aligning ourselves with the Creator of the universe, the owner of it all. Look up the following verses, noting in the right-hand column what you learn about God's reach throughout the earth.

GOD'S VAST REACH	
Verse(s)	**What We Learn about God**
1 Samuel 2:8	
Psalm 24:1	
Psalm 50:10	
Psalm 104:1-4	
Ephesians 3:20-21	

At times it feels as if we need to protect our time and our interests, to hold back on full-hearted involvement. But in the Kingdom of God, such self-preservation only serves to prove that we're not really surrendered to God.

The truth is that we will never be more successful, more stable, more secure, or more satisfied than when we are entrusting the sum of our lives to God and serving those he sent his Son to save.

3. Let me pause here and ask you to respond to the three sentences you just read. What do you think? Agree? Disagree? What assumptions, attitudes, or experiences are shaping your perspective here?

There is good news for any believer who wants to reverse course and truly trust God to risk not only putting ourselves last but also *desiring* to be last. The good news? By the power of the Holy Spirit, and with his guidance, we can do it.

✢ ✢ ✢

If the idea of becoming a servant feels foreign to you and you're not sure where to begin, let me suggest three straightforward steps you can take, starting right now:

- Spot a need.
- Set aside your own preferences.
- Surrender to God's guidance and direction.

This is, at its core, what serving is all about—observing another's interests and elevating them above your own.

Spot a Need

If you're like 99.9 percent of the people alive in the twenty-first century, your life feels full—*impossibly* full some days. You have obligations to fulfill. Errands to run. Useful habits to uphold. Meals to prepare and eat. Perhaps children to raise. On those impossibly full days, the idea of taking on someone else's problems when you are up to your neck in your own can feel like a cruel joke.

But if you've walked with Jesus for any length of time, you have probably caught wind of his seemingly upside-down approach to life. With Jesus, last is first. Least is greatest. Weakness is somehow made strong. And so it is with serving: When we choose to elevate another's interests above our own—and it *is* a choice—we begin to operate as Jesus would.

And what is the point of being a Christian, if not to live like Christ?

So take the first step: *Spot a need.* This is the easy part. You probably already do it unintentionally dozens of times a day. A friend confides in you about a struggle he or she is facing. You get a text from a family member about a situation that still isn't resolved. You see an email requesting prayer. On and on it goes, but do you ever pause to truly acknowledge the need?

4. To prove the point that you're probably already aware of some significant needs in your immediate sphere of influence, jot down below some issues that you know exist today.

Needs of my immediate family . . .

Needs of my extended family . . .

Needs of my neighbors . . .

Needs within my friend group . . .

Needs within my church . . .

Needs among my work colleagues . . .

Needs among the people who work at local establishments I frequent . . .

Needs in my city . . .

You're not attempting to solve any problems just yet. Sometimes simply sitting with the needs you see carves out greater capacity for compassion . . . compassion that God can later use.

Let's keep going.

+ + +

Set Aside Your Own Preferences

After you've taken a moment to see—and acknowledge—the needs around you, the next step is to squelch the sometimes-reflexive excuses and justifications that crop up. Ever had your inner voice holler one of these at you?

- ☐ "I can't do anything to help . . ."
- ☐ "I don't have time for that . . ."
- ☐ "They probably have all the help they need . . ."
- ☐ "Hope everything turns out okay for them . . ."
- ☐ "Not my problem . . ."

In these examples, and a hundred more I could give, the operating assumption is that we need *our* time, *our* money, *our* energy, and *our* resources for ourselves. We don't have anything left to give to others. The flaw in this belief is that "our" things aren't really *ours* at all.

5. What does 2 Corinthians 5:14-17 have to say about who we—and, by extension, all of our resources as well—belong to once we become Christians?

Once we are *in* Christ, he is also *in* us, working in us, working through us, working around us, using the life and livelihood he has given us to bless a world in need.

6. Thoughts? Reactions? Any frustrations with this train of thought?

In this progression we're working through, have you noticed that we *still* haven't solved a single need or served a single soul? We have observed the needs around us. We have reminded ourselves that all we are and all we have belongs to God, not to us. And now the third and final step: We surrender to God's guidance and direction.

Maybe he'll use us to serve a need that we see.

Maybe he won't.

The choice is up to him.

Choosing to become a servant in my church has been a truly liberating decision. I don't have to scheme and fight to get my own way. I don't have to push to the front of the line. I don't have to demand my rights.

+ + +

Surrender to God's Guidance and Direction

As we seek to become more available servants to the people around us, it's crucial to remember that the first one we serve is God. How does this play out practically in our day-to-day lives? We surrender to God's will in a given situation instead of acting from our own understanding, our own perception, and our own sense of what's ours to do.

What this means is that not every battle is ours to fight. Not every problem is ours to solve. Not every need is ours to meet.

7. Before moving ahead, think back on a time when you jumped into the fray of a problem that wasn't yours to fix.

- ☐ What was the situation?
- ☐ How were you prompted to get involved?
- ☐ What unfolded from there?
- ☐ When did you realize that your involvement was unhelpful, unwise, or unhealthy?

Record as many details of the situation as you can below and share the gist of it with your group.

A true servant wants to please his or her master. A true servant will do whatever it takes to follow both the teachings and commands of the master.

It's far better to pause and check in with God before pursuing a course of action that may not be yours to pursue at all.

+ + +

Once you spot a person in need whom you might be able to serve, and once you have pushed past your natural, self-imposed reasons for not wanting to serve, consider asking God a few of the following questions to gain clarity on what to do next:

- ☐ *How are you already solving this person's need, Father?*
- ☐ *God, what are you up to here?*
- ☐ *Is there something you'd like me to say or do?*
- ☐ *How can I help?*
- ☐ *What resources do I have that they need?*
- ☐ *If I were to help, what would you have me do?*
- ☐ *How can I show this person the love of Christ in this situation?*
- ☐ *What can I pray on behalf of this person, Lord?*

Let's practice this very thing, using one of the needs you noted on page 59. Write the need on the grid below. Then, in a posture of prayer, complete the rest of the grid, logging both the questions you're drawn to ask God and the things that come to mind as you pray.

SURRENDERING TO THE GUIDANCE OF GOD

The Need: ______________________________

My Question for God:	**God's Answer:**

As you repeatedly work through the three-step process of spotting a need, setting aside your own preferences, and surrendering to God's guidance and direction, it will become second nature to you. Over time, you'll find yourself faced with someone's need, and you'll quickly be able to ascertain what you're supposed to do. It will become *reflexive* to see—really see—another's need, step past your human-nature resistance, and check in with God to see what's yours to do.

8. Reflecting on the previous paragraph, why do you think this type of reflexive response to people's needs is critical for us to develop as followers of Jesus?

A final thought as you and your group wrap up your discussion for this session: The apostle Paul closes off his exhortation in Philippians 2 (about our having the same attitude that Christ Jesus had) by telling us where such an attitude leads. Read the following passage aloud:

> Hold firmly to the word of life; then, on the day of Christ's return, I will be proud that I did not run the race in vain and that my work was not useless. But I will rejoice even if I lose my life, pouring it out like a liquid offering to God, just like your faithful service is an offering to God. And I want all of you to share that joy. Yes, you should rejoice, and I will share your joy. (Philippians 2:16-18)

9. What word does Paul attribute to a life spent in faithful service to God?

When we commit ourselves to serving, to giving, to helping, to not only being last but also *desiring* to be last, Paul says we will know joy. Unshakeable joy. Immovable joy. Joy despite all of life's pain.

10. What do you suppose joy would mean for you? What would it look like? What would it include?

TAKING IT HOME

I want to remind you of a scene from pages 65–66 in *I Am a Christian*:

> In John 13, Jesus does something that astounds his disciples. He wraps a towel around his waist, pours water into a basin, and begins washing the disciples' feet one by one. That is, until he comes to Simon Peter. In keeping with his impetuous temperament, Peter objects: "Lord, are you going to wash my feet?" (John 13:6).
>
> Jesus calmly responds, "You don't understand now what I am doing, but someday you will" (John 13:7).
>
> When Peter still objects, Jesus does not mince words: "Unless I wash you, you won't belong to me" (John 13:8).
>
> Foot washing was dirty work, usually delegated to a house servant. Most people wore sandals on their feet, which provided some protection but didn't keep their feet from getting dirty on dusty roads and paths.
>
> It was the lowliest of tasks. It was likely very unpleasant. But it is an example of what it means to love other people by serving them.

> After Jesus washed the disciples' feet, he said, "Since I, your Lord and Teacher, have washed your feet, you ought to wash each other's feet" (John 13:14).

You probably know where this invitation is headed. I'm asking you to do the thing you're hoping I won't ask you to do: This week, wash someone else's feet. Yes, really. Literally. Humbly. With a servant's spirit.

Afterward, return here to log what the experience was like.

We can't be servants of Jesus unless we follow him as our Lord.

SESSION 6

I AM A WITNESS

Lovingly Pointing People to Christ

God will give us all the opportunities for talking about him that our obedience will allow.

[Recommended Reading]

Before you meet with your group to discuss session 6, read chapter 5, "I Am a Witness," in *I Am a Christian*. Also read the session text and complete the exercises and questions below.

PREPARING YOUR HEART

[Complete the exercises in this section on your own before attending the group meeting. These are not for group discussion but to help you begin to connect to the topics that will be discussed in this session.]

There's a reason they're referred to as "famous last words." The last words we hear from someone we know, love, and respect somehow seem weightier than other things they said. Last words reveal something of the person's highest priorities, don't they? They often tell us what was most on the person's heart and mind at the end. They speak to the person's deepest desires, greatest goals, and worthiest hopes for those he or she leaves behind.

1. If you could determine today the themes that you will leave behind, which ones would you choose? What interests, character traits, or habits do you hope people will associate with your name and your example long after you're gone? Log a few thoughts below and share one or two with your group.

____

____

____

____

Now let's take a look at what Jesus chose to communicate when he spoke *his* final words before ascending to heaven. His disciples had gathered with him and were asking whether the time had yet come for Christ to free their nation and restore the ancient kingdom. You may recall that the Hebrew people, who had long been awaiting the arrival of the Messiah, believed that he would come as a nationalist hero and a military commander who would wage war against Israel's enemies and release God's people from oppression once and for all.

The fact that Jesus came in peace, as one fighting only for truth to have its way in human hearts, was a huge disappointment to the nation of Israel. As a final act on earth, instead of trumpeting a military victory, Jesus spoke the words we find in two places in the New Testament.

Fill in the blanks below to complete the words of Acts 1:7-8.

> [Jesus] replied, "The ____________ alone has the ____________ to set those ____________ and ____________, and they are not for you to ____________. But you will receive ____________ when the ____________ ____________ comes upon you. And you will be my ____________, telling people about me everywhere—in ____________, throughout ____________, in ____________, and to the ____________ of the ____________."

Immediately after Jesus spoke these words, he ascended into heaven.

> He was taken up into a cloud while they [the disciples] were watching, and they could no longer see him. As they strained to see him rising into heaven, two white-robed men suddenly stood among them. "Men of Galilee," they said, "why are you standing here staring into heaven? Jesus has been taken from you into heaven, but someday he will return from heaven in the same way you saw him go!"
>
> ACTS 1:9-11

2. What do you think the disciples were hoping to see, hear, or otherwise experience as they strained to see Jesus rising into heaven? What do you think was on their minds?

____

____

GETTING STARTED

[After the group leader's opening remarks and review, pause for a brief prayer before watching the video.]

REFLECTION ON THE VIDEO

What is your story of faith? How will you share it with others?

GROUP DISCUSSION

[Complete the exercises in this section prior to meeting for session 6, and be prepared to share some of your answers with your group.]

Acts 1:8 is a clear restatement of the Great Commission found in Matthew 28:18-20.

1. To refresh your memory on the key points of the Great Commission, look up Matthew 28:18-20 and note below the three main actions Jesus asked his followers to take once he returned to heaven.

2. What do you think it means that Jesus chose to recap the Great Commission in his final, parting words?

3. What do his final words reveal about Jesus' heart and his core desires?

4. How do you feel about this command/commission from Jesus to share the gospel with the people you encounter day by day? Place an "x" on the continuum below to reflect where you stand.

DISTRAUGHT	OVERWHELMED	DISCOURAGED	SKEPTICAL	CURIOUS	HONORED	INSPIRED	ENERGIZED

5. What assumptions or experiences compelled you to place yourself where you did on the continuum?

I deliberately positioned this session later in the group experience because as you grow in faithfulness to practice the spiritual disciplines we discussed in previous sessions—reading God's Word, participating with a local church, serving the needs you find around you, and so forth—telling people about Jesus becomes the easiest, most natural thing you could do. If you are presently camped out on the left end of the continuum above, don't fret. As you surrender yourself to God and are formed more closely to the character of Jesus, you will naturally want to share the Good News with others. Witnessing will become easier.

At its core, what we call "witnessing" is simply agreeing with Jesus that his commission to all believers really is great, really is important, and really is worthy of our time and energy and care. Let's look at why witnessing matters so much and how we as believers can get it done.

Why Witnessing Matters

The fact that Jesus commands us to share our faith ought to be enough motivation for us to follow through, but there is another key reason that we should witness to a world in need.

6. What do you learn in John 14:6 about what that reason might be?

7. How does Jesus' claim of exclusivity square with the popular notion that there are many ways to get to God and many ways to define who or what God is?

To *witness* means to report of what one has seen or heard; a Christian witness is one whose life and actions testify to the value and effect of faith.

8. What do you make of the vast gulf in understanding between what the world believes to be true and what Jesus says is true?

Before You Witness

As you work through the next section, keep in mind two assurances that Christ has given us as his witnesses throughout the earth:

Assurance #1: You have *spiritual authority* to witness on his behalf. You don't have to depend on your own knowledge, wisdom, or authority. You have been given authority by the King of kings and Lord of lords. Go with the confidence of Christ.

9. What encouragement do you take from the knowledge that you have spiritual authority as you witness on behalf of Christ?

Assurance #2: You have *spiritual accompaniment* by the Holy Spirit and therefore do not go alone. You'll recall that Jesus' final statement to his disciples when issuing the Great Commission was to say, "Be sure of this: I am with you always, even to the end of the age" (Matthew 28:20). In *The Message* version, the Lord's reminder reads this way: "I'll be with you as you do this, day after day after day, right up to the end of the age."

10. How might it change your daily interactions to know that God's Spirit is always with you, guiding you as you engage with people in spiritual conversations?

God gives you *everything* you need to be a witness for Christ. You don't need human eloquence or human-centered courage. As you share the gospel, continually rely on Jesus to be with you and to empower you. He will answer that prayer every time with a resounding yes.

The Three Rs of Witnessing

As you think about witnessing to people, I'd like you to keep three Rs in mind:

Reach out: Simply look up from your life, your struggles, your concerns (and your phone!) to notice other people. Upon noticing them, *engage*. Smile. Say hello. Ask a question. Ask another question after that.

Relate: Get to know their stories. And in time, be prepared to share yours.

Request: Invite them to meet you for a cup of coffee, to come over for lunch, or to attend church with you sometime soon. If you're going for a hike on Tuesday night, invite them to join you. If you're running some errands on Saturday, invite them to come along. If you're serving at church on Sunday, invite them to come chat while you pass out flyers or greet people as they arrive and then sit with you during the worship service.

11. Describe a time when you've seen the 3 R method of witnessing have an impact in the life of someone you know.

+ + +

Once you enter into a spiritual conversation with someone you've reached out to, it's critical for you to know how to tell two stories: the story of God's grace and the story of how God's grace has affected you.

The Story of God's Grace

One of my favorite ways to share the story of God's grace—the gospel message—is called "Three Circles," a concept created by Pastor Jimmy Scroggins, who serves with a church in West Palm Beach, Florida. With Pastor Jimmy's permission, I'll share an abbreviated version of the approach here.[1]

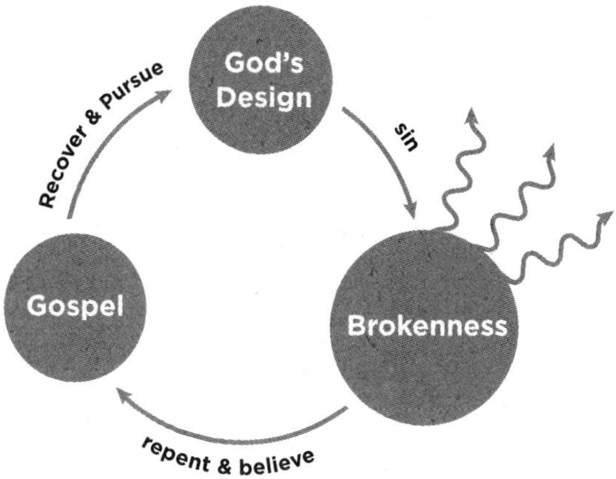

What is "the gospel"? The word *gospel* simply means "good news." When you "share the gospel," then, you are simply telling someone about the good news of God's grace, afforded to us by Jesus' sacrifice on the cross.

Step 1: God's Design

The Bible tells us that God has a plan for each of our lives, and that that plan is *good*. If we follow God's design, we experience God's blessing.

Step 2: Sin

We all have a tendency to depart from God's design. Isaiah 53:6 says, "All of us, like

[1] For more information about the Three Circles, see https://www.namb.net/evangelism/3circles/. For a video of Pastor Jimmy walking through the tool step-by-step, see https://vimeo.com/227782208.

sheep, have strayed away." We've all gone our own way. The Bible calls this tendency *sin*.

Step 3: Brokenness

When we sin against God, we wind up in a place called *brokenness*. Here we experience guilt, shame, emptiness, regret, and pain. God seems far away, and because this distance is awful, we try in our own power to fix the brokenness we feel.

Step 4: Escaping the Pain

In response to our brokenness, we try to do better. We try to *be* better. We work to make more money, build stronger muscles, or launch a new relationship. We think new habits will fix what's broken. New clothes. A new car. But in the end, nothing works. We're still broken and far from God.

Step 5: Repent and Believe in the Gospel

Eventually we realize that the change we seek must come from somewhere else, from *someone* else. That someone is God. John 3:16 says, "For this is how God loved the world: He gave his one and only Son, so that everyone who believes in him will not perish but have eternal life." When we trust in the power of God—and the finished work of his Son, Jesus—instead of relying on our own strength, we are saved eternally from brokenness. We can return to God's original design.

Step 6: Recover and Pursue God's Design

When we repent of our sins and quit relying on our own will and ways and strength, God gives us the opportunity to pursue his plans for us once again. From the moment of salvation, we get to walk with God.

The Story of God's Grace and You

The second story you need to be able to tell is how God's grace has had an impact on your life. A simple and straightforward way to shape such a story is to think of who you were before you surrendered your life to Jesus, how that act of surrender came to be, and who you are today.

If your story of salvation is one of gradual awakening, you might think in terms of how you came to understand your need for Christ and the difference it has made to follow him.

Complete the grid below by filling in the highlights of your own experience. An example has been provided.

MY STORY OF GOD'S GRACE		
Who I Was before I Met Jesus	**How I Met Jesus**	**Who I Am Today**
Example: stingy, self-consumed.	Friend at work invited me to come to a church retreat. I prayed to receive Christ on the final day.	Generous. More others-focused day by day.

The more you tell your story, the more succinct it will become. But for now, simply getting the facts down on paper will help form the skeleton of the story in your mind and heart.

Praying Your Way Through

A final word as you conclude this session: Remember that witnessing is an act of service in the life of someone you care about deeply enough to tell them the truth. Be careful to rely on divine guidance instead of your own insight as you share the gospel.

The entirety of session 7 is devoted to the topic of prayer, but as it relates specifically to witnessing, let me give you five areas to pray about before you begin reaching out to people with the hope of Christ. Below each of the following five categories, I invite you to respond with ideas for how you might begin implementing such prayers this week.

Pray for opportunities.

Ask God to show you people who need hope and love, and ask that such people will cross your path.

Pray for non-Christians.

Ask God to open your heart, especially to people who don't yet know him. Pray by name for those you believe are living far from God.

Pray that people would say yes to the gospel.

Ask God to prompt people to say yes to your invitation to church, yes to knowing more about Jesus, yes to receiving grace in their own lives.

Pray for your own boldness.

Ask God to help you overcome any fears or insecurities that would keep you from sharing his love courageously and confidently.

Pray for your pastor and church leaders to be witnesses. Ask God to help the leaders of your church discern spiritual opportunities and seize them.

TAKING IT HOME

Between now and when your group convenes for session 7, witness to someone. Share God's good news of grace. Share how that good news turned your life around. Share your passion for Jesus. Trust God that he will cause that interaction to bear fruit.

Even if you only practice witnessing on your fully-devoted-to-Jesus friend or family member, wonderful strides will be made as you hear your own voice put words to the marvelous change Jesus has made in your life.

So, share.

Share the gospel boldly.

Share the gospel this week.

SESSION 7

I AM A PRAYER WARRIOR

Asking God for What He Already Wants to Give

Prayer is our spiritual weapon as we fight for and along with God in this great battle.

[Recommended Reading]

Before you meet with your group to discuss session 7, read chapter 6, "I Am a Prayer Warrior," in *I Am a Christian*. Also read the session text and complete the exercises and questions below.

PREPARING YOUR HEART

[Complete the exercises in this section on your own before attending the group meeting. These are not for group discussion but to help you begin to connect to the topics that will be discussed in this session.]

When was the last time you put up a fight? Someone or something was so important to you that you just couldn't let the thing go. You stayed on hold for *hours*, waiting to talk to that customer-service rep. You stayed up long past your bedtime, sticking with the conversation to be sure you made your point. You stayed the course with a work project you should have bailed on, just to prove you could get it done.

1. Write about the last time you fought to get something done. Log the key points of the experience below and share them with your group.

Even those of us who are introverted and relatively conflict-avoidant can feel that fighting spirit rise in us from time to time. Something happens, and the next thing we know, we're going toe-to-toe with whoever or whatever is standing between us and the justice we think we deserve. Spiritually speaking, there is a clear call in the New Testament for followers of Jesus to be people of peace; people who bring peace with them wherever they go; people who, as far as it depends on them, choose to "live in peace with everyone" (Romans 12:18).

And yet equally true is that the apostle Paul assures us that we're at *war*. That we're in a *fight*. And that the spoils of that battle are our very souls.

Sometimes, that fighting spirit is a God-given thing.

Look up the following verses, noting what you learn about the battle we're in.

THE BATTLE BELIEVERS ARE IN	
Verse(s):	**Insights Regarding the War We're In:**
Romans 8:35-39	
2 Corinthians 10:4-5	
Ephesians 6:10-12	

2 Thessalonians 3:3	
James 4:1-7	
1 Peter 5:6-9	

2. How do you balance the calling to be a person of peace with the very real fact that, as a Christian, you're at war?

GETTING STARTED

[After the group leader's opening remarks and review, pause for a brief prayer before watching the video.]

REFLECTION ON THE VIDEO

When have you seen prayer transform your life?

GROUP DISCUSSION

[Complete the exercises in this section prior to meeting for session 7, and be prepared to share some of your answers with your group.]

In Romans 7, Paul gives us one of the greatest testimonies of being in a spiritual war ever written. Look up verses 15 through 20, filling in the blanks below as you go.

I don't really ________________ myself, for I want
to do what is ________________, but I don't do it.
Instead, I do what I ________________. But if I know
that what I am doing is ________________, this
shows that I agree that the law is ________________.
So I am not the one doing ________________; it is
________________ living in me that does it. And I
know that ________________ good lives in me, that
is, in my ________________ nature. I want to do
what is ________________, but I can't. I want to do
what is ________________, but I don't. I don't want
to do what is ________________, but I do it anyway.
But if I do what I ________________ want to do,
I am not really the one doing ________________;
it is sin ________________ in me that does it.
(Romans 7:15-20)

1. Can you relate to what Paul is talking about? Describe a time when you didn't do what you knew was right or did the very thing you had been determined not to do. If appropriate, share it with your group.

2. Looking back on the experience, what do you make of your own unwillingness or inability to act wisely? How do you make sense of this reality that we all face from time to time?

+ + +

We know from Genesis 1:26 that we were created in God's image. We know from Jeremiah 29:11 that God has plans for us that are "for good and not for disaster, to give [us] a future and a hope." And we know from Romans 8:28 that God is causing "everything to work together for the good of those who love God and are called according to his purpose for them."

These are comforting assurances, to be sure.

And yet what is also true is that between our birth, when we come into the world as image-bearers of God, and our death, when God's ultimate plan for our souls as believers in Jesus comes to fruition, we can experience a *lot* of distress, disappointment, and pain.

The question is this: Does it have to be this way?

3. What does Paul imply in Ephesians 6:11 that you and I are capable of doing? Look up the verse and record below what you find.

Given how often you and I enter into the frustrating cycle Paul talked about earlier—doing what we don't want to do, not doing what we know is right—it might be surprising that here in Ephesians 6:11, Paul says in no uncertain terms that it really is possible for us to "stand firm against all strategies of the devil."

We can stand firm.

+ + +

Ephesians 6 is best known for its "armor of God" section, in which Paul lays out the spiritual coverings we should apply to our lives to fend off Satan's schemes. When we do, Paul says, we will be found "standing firm" after the battle, which is an outcome you and I both are wise to desire.

4. Using Ephesians 6:14-17 as a reference, label each part of armor noted on the image below with its spiritual purpose or function.

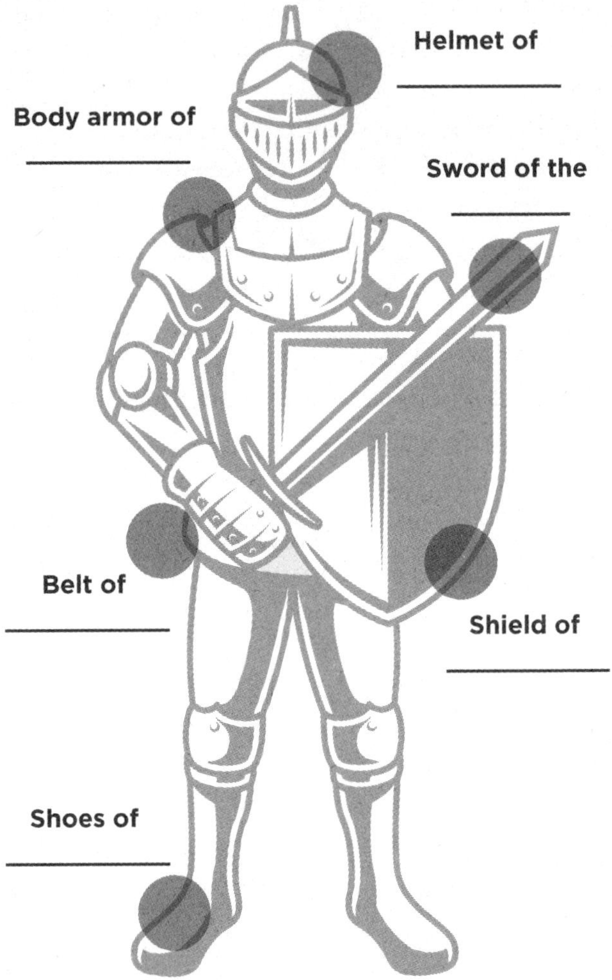

Put on the Armor of God

Ephesians 6:14-17

5. Following Paul's description of the six pieces of armor (the *what*), he reminds us of the *how*. What counsel does he offer in Ephesians 6:18 regarding how we can stay "armored up"?

____

____

Remember, this is Paul writing, the same person who told us about that ridiculously annoying human-nature propensity to do what we don't want to do and neglect to do the very thing we desire. Here, it's as if he's saying, "Friends, listen up. I've found the way to reverse that deadly cycle."

The answer, it turns out, is *prayer*.

\+ \+ \+

6. Before we move into a discussion on the purpose and power of prayer, let me ask you this: How would you define prayer to someone who had never prayed before? Do any of the explanations below ring true to your experience? What ideas would you add to the mix?

- ☐ Prayer is conversation with God.
- ☐ Prayer is laying down my burdens.
- ☐ Prayer is agreeing with God.
- ☐ Prayer is worshiping God.
- ☐ Prayer is making requests of God.
- ☐ Prayer is asking God for help.
- ☐ Prayer is telling God my needs.
- ☐ Prayer is trusting God.
- ☐ Prayer is voicing concerns to God.
- ☐ Prayer is confession.
- ☐ Prayer is ______________________.
- ☐ Prayer is ______________________.

☐ Prayer is ______________________.
☐ Prayer is ______________________.

Based on the word that Paul uses in Ephesians 6:18 when he exhorts us to "Pray in the Spirit at all times and on every occasion," any and all of the above descriptions are true. Why? Because prayer in the way that Paul defined it means to interact intimately with God.

So when we describe someone as a "prayer warrior," what we're saying is that the way he or she approaches the very real battle we face is by *choosing to pause and pray.*

To *pray* simply means to interact intimately with God.

If you're feeling impotent these days in the battle that's been waged for your attention and your affection, let me encourage you for a moment: Most likely, the issue is prayer.

Prayer is not hard. But it's easy to neglect.

7. Do you see these two truths play out in your life? If so, how? First, what does it mean that prayer is "not hard"?

8. Second, why is prayer so easy to neglect? Log below a handful of reasons that come to mind.

In the remainder of this session, I want to draw your attention to a fresh perspective on prayer's purpose and power. I'll also give you an opportunity to *not* neglect prayer this week.

To Pray Is to Acknowledge the War We're In

In 2 Kings 6:8-17, we see an incredible scene unfold. By way of context, two powerful factions are at war: the nations of Israel and Aram.

The king of Aram devised a plan to ambush Israel's king and capture the Hebrew people and their land for himself, but a man of God named Elisha repeatedly divulged his plans to the king of Israel. The king of Aram was enraged.

Aram's king called his military officers together and grilled them: "Tell me, who is leaking information to the king of Israel? Who is the spy in our ranks?" (verse 11, MSG).

Eventually one of his men spoke up. "It's not any of us. It's Elisha the prophet in Israel. He tells the king of Israel everything you say" (verse 12, MSG).

Ah, so *Elisha* was the problem.

Well, then, Elisha would have to pay.

"Go and find out where he is," the king said. "I'll send someone and capture him" (verse 13, MSG).

Shortly thereafter, the king "dispatched horses and chariots, an impressive fighting force" (verse 14, MSG) to Dothan, where Elisha was.

The next morning, Elisha's servant woke up and went outside to find a ring of Aram's horses and chariots surrounding the city. "Oh, master!" he shouted. "What shall we do?" (verse 15, MSG).

To which Elisha replied, "Don't worry about it—there are more on our side than on their side," (verse 16, MSG).

Then, in verse 17, we read the following words: "Elisha prayed, 'O GOD, open his eyes and let him see.'"

9. Look up 2 Kings 6:17. How did God respond to Elisha's prayer?

---

10. How do you suppose God would respond if you made a habit of making that same request—not only for others but for yourself, as well?

+ + +

You and I both experience manifestations of spiritual warfare every day. Our boss makes another impossible request, and internally we're filled with rage. Our spouse forgets to take care of a task, and we take it as a meaningful slight. Our pastor makes a statement we disagree with, and we contemplate ditching the church. The neighbors don't stop their dog from barking, and without thinking it through we storm out the door toward their home.

> Something happens, and we feel provoked.
> Someone does something, and we take offense.
> A situation unfolds, and we just can't take it.
> Circumstances tempt us, and we too quickly
> cave to sin.

11. What are some ways you've felt the wearying effects of spiritual warfare recently? What battles have you been fighting?

Though it's true that we will be confronted with all sorts of trials and temptations in this world, it's also true that because of Jesus' work on the cross, the war has already been won. Just as God's army stood guard over Elisha's seemingly desperate situation, his army stands guard over you and me.

And just as Elisha prayed that his servant would have eyes to see those protective forces, we, too, can ask for God's victory to be made plain.

12. How might seeing God's victorious forces surrounding you help you deal with the pressures you face?

You don't have to give way to anger.
You don't have to cave to fear.
You don't have to act on temptation.
You don't have to worry or fret.
You don't have to assert power over other people.
You don't have to be offended.
You don't have to carry regret.

When you pray for God's victory in your life, you acknowledge both the battle you're in and the fact that the war has already been won.

To Pray Is to Fight against Darkness

While prayer is learning to *see* differently, it holds even greater power. When we see things from a fresh perspective, we gain new vision for how to act.

13. Practically speaking, when have you experienced a situation where once you had the full story, you changed your perspective on why someone acted a certain way?

- ☐ You wondered why your child was failing math until you learned that his vision had taken a nosedive, and he could no longer read the whiteboard at school.
- ☐ You wondered why your colleague wasn't showing much interest in the company's sales contest, until you learned she'd resigned to take another job.
- ☐ You wondered why your friend had quit reaching out, until you learned that she was going through an agonizing divorce.

Describe a time when added context helped you make better sense of things.

When we have the full story, we can better handle disappointing turns of events. When we see the broader context, we know better how to respond.

And so it is with prayer: When we ask God to show us how he's working all around us, things may feel a little less mysterious.

✝ ✝ ✝

Let's look at how this works.

For the next several minutes, log in the left-hand column below any present concerns, struggles, sources of anxiety, and fears you are facing. Then, in the right-hand column, write down the effects these are having in your life. An example has been provided.

MY PRESENT PERSONAL BATTLES	
Nature of the Battle	**Effect(s) It's Having in My Life**
Example: Dissatisfaction in my marriage	Little quality time spent together in months. Every conversation turns into an argument. My fuse is getting shorter, and my patience is wearing thin. Having trouble sleeping. Losing hope.

14. Now for an honest question: For which of the struggles noted above have you persevered in prayer? Go ahead and circle the challenges you've regularly brought before God.

In a study of the state of the church last year, the Barna Group reported that just under seven in ten Americans "prayed weekly."[2] Praying once a week is a far cry from the frequency the apostle Paul encourages in Ephesians 6:18. There, as you may recall, he said for us to:

> Pray in the Spirit at ______________ times and on ______________ occasion.

15. Why do you suppose *constancy in prayer* is key to conquering the disheartening wartime effects we face?

[2] "Signs of Decline & Hope Among Key Metrics of Faith," Barna: State of the Church 2020, March 4, 2020, barna.com/research/changing-state-of-the-church.

When you and I choose to give ourselves over to prayer rather than to negative emotions such as frustration, anxiety, fear, anger, and defensiveness, we remind ourselves that even when our circumstances may not immediately change, our *perspectives* on them can.

To Pray Is to Fight for the Light

In *I Am a Christian*, I cite a host of topics we can pray about each day as a type of proactive wartime maneuver—a frontal assault on the enemy, you could say.

16. As you consider the following topics, note the thoughts that spring to mind about specific requests you could make to God.

Praying for my witness

Praying for my pastor

Praying for the lost

Praying for the hurting

Praying for unity

The thoughts that come to mind as you scroll through your various spheres of influence are the fuel for a vibrant prayer life. They are the raw materials of intimacy with your heavenly Father. They are the tone-setters for life-giving days.

Remember, God longs to give us good things, as a devoted parent to a beloved child. Ask him for the change you long to see in your world. Trust that he will provide.

TAKING IT HOME

Between now and your final session, I encourage you to keep a prayer journal, either the one provided at the back of this guide or another of your choosing. The approach is straightforward:

- Whenever you are compelled to pray—either because a negative situation confronts you or because you've chosen to proactively come before God—note the day or date when you are praying. Note the topic or person you are praying for. And note your specific prayer request.
- After you've logged your prayer request, ask God to help you see his hand at work in this specific area. Watch for his activity—this may be what Paul is referring to in Ephesians 6:18 when he tells us to "stay alert" as we persist in prayer.
- As you receive answers from God to the requests you have made, note the date.

As with all habits, what seems cumbersome and unwieldly at first starts to feel reflexive and natural over time. Give yourself grace as you begin this new practice. Soon enough, you will be an outright prayer warrior. You will see God's divine movement. And you will join him in that good work.

SESSION 8

I AM A CHRISTIAN

Living Life That Is Truly Life

We are Christians because of what Christ has done for us. We respond by growing as Christians and doing what God desires.

[Recommended Reading]

Before you meet with your group to discuss session 8, read chapter 7, "I Am a Christian," in *I Am a Christian*. Also read the session text and complete the exercises and questions below.

PREPARING YOUR HEART

[Complete the exercises in this section on your own before attending the group meeting. These are not for group discussion but to help you begin to connect to the topics that will be discussed in this session.]

It is said that the workplace concept known as "planned obsolescence" originated in the automobile industry. In the early 1920s, so many people had already purchased cars that automobile manufacturers such as Ford and Chevrolet were struggling to hit their sales goals. Then someone in the industry had a bright idea: Why not upgrade their vehicles a bit, give them a little facelift, and convince the consumer that even though their current vehicle was working just fine, they just *had* to have the latest and greatest model?

The idea stuck, and in 1923 Chevrolet rolled out a completely restyled exterior that covered inner technology nearly a decade old. From that moment on, every driver in the world has been tempted to trade in a perfectly good car for one whose primary selling point was "It's new."

Disposability is a too-common trend. Over time, our vehicles give out—or at least go out of style. Our houses fall into a state of disrepair. Our smartphones get sluggish. Our clothing wears thin. Is there anything that will hold up over the long haul? Is anything made to last?

1. When have you come face-to-face with the truth that so much about our present reality wasn't made to last?

At the end of Paul's famous writing about love in 1 Corinthians 13, he says this: "Three things will last forever . . ." (verse 13).

What three things does he cite?

2. Why might the order of these three things matter, in your view? In other words, why would having faith necessarily need to come before holding fast to hope, and how does the practice of holding fast to hope fuel our ability to choose to love?

As we'll discover in this session, it is our *faith* in Jesus Christ that inspires *hope* for a future spent in God's presence. And it is this confidence that expands our ability to *love*—to love God, to love ourselves, and to love each person he puts in our path.

GETTING STARTED

[After the group leader's opening remarks and review, pause for a brief prayer before watching the video.]

REFLECTION ON THE VIDEO

Which Christian traits will you practice in the coming months?

GROUP DISCUSSION

[Complete the exercises in this section prior to meeting for session 8, and be prepared to share some of your answers with your group.]

To begin, respond to the statement above: "It is our *faith* in Jesus Christ that inspires *hope* for a future spent in God's presence. And it is this confidence that expands our ability to *love*—to love God, to love ourselves, and to love each person he puts in our path."

1. Answer the following questions in your group.

- Do you agree or disagree with this progression? Why?

- Do you think it's possible to possess one of these elements but not the other two?

- If this progression were true, why would Paul sum up his assertion with the idea that the "greatest of these is love" (see 1 Corinthians 13:13)? Wouldn't *faith* be the most important element, since the progression begins with that?

Regardless of the order of these three manifestations of the Christian life, they are the three primary markers of one who is earnestly following Jesus. What's more, as we invest ourselves in the life of our local church congregations, faith, hope, and love become the primary markers of a healthy church.

Christians Have Greater Faith

I make the statement in *I Am a Christian* that the believers who formed the early church were people of great faith. "The supernatural work of the Holy Spirit moved these new believers into a community of believers."

And that community *demonstrated* their faith.

This faith was shown in their courage to trust God's presence, in their witnessing of miraculous signs and wonders, in their cheerful giving of their possessions, and in their sharing of the gospel with people who weren't yet saved.

2. How has your faith affected your ability to trust God's presence, witness miraculous signs and wonders, give generously, and share the gospel with others?

Faith means having conviction regarding God's truthfulness and our reliance on Christ for salvation.

Curiously, when we renew our faith in Jesus, we simultaneously renew our commitment to participation in a local church.

3. What do you make of this correlation? Have you ever experienced this dynamic to be true in your own life? Write down your thoughts to share with the group.

4. To wrap up this discussion on faith, answer the following two-part question with the other members in your group:

   - How is the faith of others in my church encouraging me these days?

   - How might my faith encourage others who are part of my church?

Something powerful takes place when God's people come together in faith. It happened two thousand years ago. And it is still happening today.

Christians Have Greater Hope

The second of the three things that remain, Paul says, is *hope.*

5. How would you define hope, in your own words?

6. Describe a time when you have most needed a sense of hope. What were the circumstances involved, and how did you find the hope you needed to overcome the obstacles you faced?

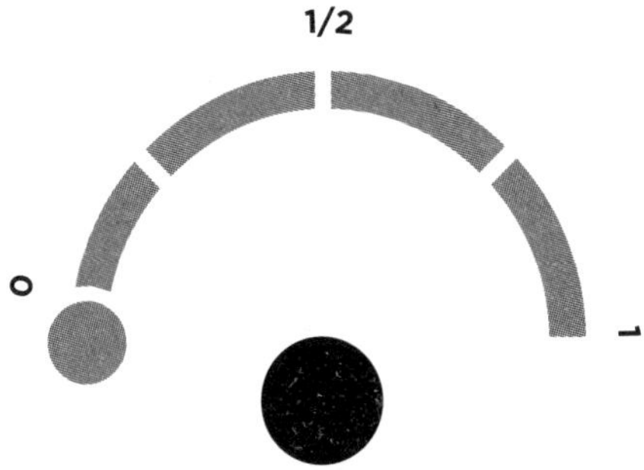

7. How full is your "hope tank" these days? Note your answer on the image above and then explain your rating to your group.

Hope means pleasurable anticipation; favorable and confident expectation; the ready prospect of good.

8. What affects your sense of hopefulness day by day? What assumptions, insights, or experiences shape your answer here?

In *I Am a Christian*, I note that our sense of individual hope as believers rises and falls in direct proportion to our involvement with a local church. As we participate in the life of a local church, our sense of hopefulness goes up. As we pull away, our sense of hopefulness goes down.

9. How have you seen this correlation play out in your own life? Why do you think this dynamic exists?

____

____

____

Instead, you must worship Christ as Lord of your life. And if someone asks about your hope as a believer, always be ready to explain it. (1 Peter 3:15)

10. What does 1 Peter 3:15 (see sidebar) say is our responsibility as believers regarding *hope*?

We must ______________
be ______________ to
______________ it.

How would you explain the hope that lies within *you*?

The apostle Paul had to answer this question when the stakes were impossibly high. He'd been asked to testify before King Agrippa, the son of the man who had killed the apostle James and imprisoned the apostle Peter.

Paul had been brought into Agrippa's chambers in chains, having been arrested on charges of desecrating the Temple, a crime he did not commit. Because Paul was a Roman citizen by birth, he was allowed this last-ditch opportunity to explain himself—and save himself from being executed by the state. Acts 26 begins with Agrippa saying to Paul, "You may speak in your defense."

Have a group member read aloud Acts 26:1-32, which appears below. In the passage, note the following movements as you come across them:

- ☐ Movement I: Paul's greeting and initial plea.
- ☐ Movement II: Paul's "before" story; who he was before he knew Jesus Christ.
- ☐ Movement III: Paul's encounter with Jesus.
- ☐ Movement IV: Paul's "after" story; who he became upon encountering Christ.
- ☐ Movement V: Paul's invitation to King Agrippa.

Then Agrippa said to Paul, "You may speak in your defense."

So Paul, gesturing with his hand, started his defense: "I am fortunate, King Agrippa, that you are the one hearing my defense today against all these accusations made by the Jewish leaders, for I know you are an expert on all Jewish customs and controversies. Now please listen to me patiently!

"As the Jewish leaders are well aware, I was given a thorough Jewish training from my earliest childhood among my own people and in Jerusalem. If they would admit it, they know that I have been a member of the Pharisees, the strictest sect of our religion. Now I am on trial because of my hope in the fulfillment of God's promise made to our ancestors. In fact, that is why the twelve tribes of Israel zealously worship God night and day, and they share the same hope I have. Yet, Your Majesty, they accuse me for having this hope! Why does it seem incredible to any of you that God can raise the dead?

"I used to believe that I ought to do everything I could to oppose the very name of Jesus the Nazarene. Indeed, I did just that in Jerusalem. Authorized by the leading priests, I caused many believers there to be sent to prison. And I cast my vote against them when they were condemned to death. Many times I had them punished in the synagogues to get them to curse Jesus. I was so violently opposed to them that I even chased them down in foreign cities.

"One day I was on such a mission to Damascus, armed with the authority and commission of the leading priests. About noon, Your Majesty, as I was on the road, a light from heaven brighter than the sun shone down on me and my companions. We all fell down, and I heard a voice saying to me in Aramaic, 'Saul, Saul, why are you persecuting me? It is useless for you to fight against my will.'

"'Who are you, lord?' I asked.

"And the Lord replied, 'I am Jesus, the one you are persecuting. Now get to your feet! For I have appeared to you to appoint you as my servant and witness. Tell people that you have seen me, and tell them what I will show you in the future. And I will rescue you from both your own people and the Gentiles. Yes, I am sending you to the Gentiles to open their eyes, so they may turn from darkness to light and from the power of Satan to God. Then they will receive forgiveness for their sins and be given a place among God's people, who are set apart by faith in me.'

"And so, King Agrippa, I obeyed that vision from heaven. I preached first to those in Damascus, then in Jerusalem and throughout all Judea, and also to the Gentiles, that all must repent of their sins and turn to God—and prove they have changed by the good things they do. Some Jews arrested me in the Temple for preaching this, and they tried to kill me. But God has protected me right up to this present time so I can testify to everyone, from the least to the greatest. I teach nothing except what the prophets and Moses said would happen—that the Messiah would suffer and be the first to rise from the dead, and in this way announce God's light to Jews and Gentiles alike."

Suddenly, Festus shouted, "Paul, you are insane. Too much study has made you crazy!"

But Paul replied, "I am not insane, Most Excellent Festus. What I am saying is the sober truth. And King Agrippa knows

> about these things. I speak boldly, for I am sure these events are all familiar to him, for they were not done in a corner! King Agrippa, do you believe the prophets? I know you do—"
>
> Agrippa interrupted him. "Do you think you can persuade me to become a Christian so quickly?"
>
> Paul replied, "Whether quickly or not, I pray to God that both you and everyone here in this audience might become the same as I am, except for these chains."
>
> Then the king, the governor, Bernice, and all the others stood and left. As they went out, they talked it over and agreed, "This man hasn't done anything to deserve death or imprisonment."
>
> And Agrippa said to Festus, "He could have been set free if he hadn't appealed to Caesar."

You and I probably won't ever be asked to give an answer for the hope that lies within us while we're standing in chains before the leader of the country in which we live. Nor will that answer include the fact that we once murdered Christians out of a sense of religious duty. But the point remains: As often as we are able to speak to the fact that regardless of our circumstances we remain people of great hope, we should.

More to the point: *We must.*

11. Look back at your own before-and-after story, which you logged on page 77 of this guide. How does your story provide you with a constant flow of hope?

In the same way that Paul wished *change* rather than *chains* for King Agrippa, as we tell our own stories we must realize we have the opportunity to help set people free.

Christians Have Greater Love

The three things that will always remain?

Faith.
Hope.
And then this: *love.*

Love. Is there a single word in the English language with more diverse and even convoluted meanings than the word *love*?

You can love pizza and love your spouse.

You can love roller coasters and love your child.

You can love pro football and love Jesus.

How can this all be love?

In the New Testament, we are handed a clear definition of the kind of love that God is referring to when he tells us to be people of love. In Greek, *agape* love means benevolent affection expressing the essential nature of God, known by the actions it prompts.

12. What are some observations you make about love based on this definition?

In his classic writing on the subject of love—1 Corinthians 13:4-7—Paul cites fifteen characteristics that help us recognize whether or not we are living as loving people.

As a self-diagnostic on your current attitudes and behaviors, rate yourself on the following lineup using a scale of 1 (rarely true) to 5 (almost always true).

I am patient.	1	2	3	4	5
I am kind.	1	2	3	4	5
I am not jealous.	1	2	3	4	5
I am not boastful.	1	2	3	4	5
I am not proud.	1	2	3	4	5
I am not rude.	1	2	3	4	5
I do not demand my own way.	1	2	3	4	5
I am not irritable.	1	2	3	4	5
I keep no record of being wronged.	1	2	3	4	5
I do not rejoice about injustice.	1	2	3	4	5
I rejoice when truth wins out.	1	2	3	4	5
I never give up on those I love.	1	2	3	4	5
I never lose faith on behalf of those I love.	1	2	3	4	5
I am always hopeful.	1	2	3	4	5
I endure through every circumstance.	1	2	3	4	5

+ + +

13. Looking back at the New Testament definition of love on page 108 of this guide, what is the only way that love can be known?

Love is known by the ____________________ it prompts.

Based on this truth, for any of the characteristics of love that you might be struggling to manifest (as noted on the rating scale you just completed), how do you suppose you could increase your ability to love well?

14. Sit with this idea for a moment. What are three actions you will take this week to better allow God's love to manifest itself through you?

+ + +

When we choose to live lives marked by the three enduring aspects of a Christ-following life—faith, hope, and love—we experience what the Bible calls "life that is truly life" (1 Timothy 6:19, NIV).

15. What do you think "life that is truly life" would look like for you?

Before ending this final session, take a few minutes together as a group to talk about your experience in this study. What has been helpful to you? What next steps are you committed to? How can your group members encourage you as you continue to grow in your identity in Christ?

Close by praying for each other's continued growth.

TAKING IT HOME

To assess your current progress in the various aspects of Christianity you have explored during this group experience, I invite you to pray through the seven "I Am" statements below.

Sit with the questions that appear underneath each category, either silently answering them in your mind and heart or simply letting them float on your thoughts for a beat.

Ask God to help you examine yourself to see if your faith is genuine. Ask him to bring divine strength to any weak areas in your life and to work through you to impact your generation for good.

Commitment #1: I Am a Believer

- ☐ Is Jesus truly Lord of my life?
- ☐ Is my primary identity that I am a follower of Jesus Christ?
- ☐ Can I clearly articulate my spiritual beliefs to someone who doesn't yet know Jesus?
- ☐ Am I passionate about my relationship with Jesus?

Commitment #2: I Am a Church Member

- ☐ Do I long to adore the bride of Christ as much as Jesus does?
- ☐ Am I faithful to participate with a local church?
- ☐ Do I seek to serve the church more than I seek to be served by the church?
- ☐ Do I regularly give to my local church?
- ☐ Do I regularly pray for my church leaders?
- ☐ Am I known as a unifier in my church?

Commitment #3: I Am a Disciple

- ☐ Of all the people I follow, is Jesus preeminent among them?
- ☐ Of all the voices I listen to, is God's clearest in my mind?
- ☐ Am I faithful to read my Bible daily?
- ☐ Do I readily practice forgiving those who have wronged me?
- ☐ Do I regularly pray for my own spiritual development?
- ☐ Am I faithful to disciple others even as I am discipled?

Commitment #4: I Am a Servant

- ☐ Do I regularly put the needs of others before my own?
- ☐ Am I content to be last?
- ☐ Do I seek to please God by serving those he sent his Son to save?
- ☐ Do I freely give to people in need, knowing that my resources belong to God and not to me?
- ☐ Do others know me as someone who serves with joy?

Commitment #5: I Am a Witness

- ☐ Is *love* the primary emotion I feel toward people who aren't yet following Christ?
- ☐ Am I unashamed—and even proud—of the gospel message?
- ☐ Do I believe in my heart that receiving Jesus is the only way to be saved?
- ☐ Do I share the gospel in such a way that people can see that I'm walking in the Spirit?
- ☐ Do I regularly pray for spiritual doors to open that I may walk through?

Commitment #6: I Am a Prayer Warrior

- ☐ Do I see myself as a prayer warrior?
- ☐ Do others see me as a prayer warrior?
- ☐ Do others regularly ask me to pray for them? Am I faithful to follow through?
- ☐ Do I respond with prayer when unfortunate events unfold in my life?
- ☐ Do I proactively pray for my witness, my pastor, people who are hurting, people who are lost, and for unity in the church?

Commitment #7: I Am a Christian

- ☐ Am I known as a faithful person?
- ☐ Am I known as a hopeful person?
- ☐ Am I known as a loving person?

PRAYER JOURNAL

When you feel compelled to pray, note the date and the person or situation for which you are praying. Then write your specific prayer request in the space provided. As you pray, ask God to help you see his hand at work. Watch for his response in the days and weeks ahead, "staying alert," as Paul advises in Ephesians 6:18, as you persist in prayer. As you receive answers from God, note the date.

Day/Date: ________ **Praying for:** ________________________
Fulfilled? ❐ **Date fulfilled:** ________________

Prayer request: ________________________________

____

____

____

____

Day/Date: ________ **Praying for:** ________________________
Fulfilled? ❐ **Date fulfilled:** ________________

Prayer request: ________________________________

____

____

____

____

Day/Date: __________ Praying for: ______________________________
Fulfilled? ❒ Date fulfilled: ______________________

Prayer request: ____

____

____

____

____

Day/Date: __________ Praying for: ______________________________
Fulfilled? ❒ Date fulfilled: ______________________

Prayer request: ____

____

____

____

____

Day/Date: __________ Praying for: ______________________________
Fulfilled? ❒ Date fulfilled: ______________________

Prayer request: ____

____

____

____

____

Day/Date: __________ Praying for: ______________________________

Fulfilled? ❒ Date fulfilled: ______________________

Prayer request: ____

____

____

____

____

Day/Date: __________ Praying for: ______________________________

Fulfilled? ❒ Date fulfilled: ______________________

Prayer request: ____

____

____

____

____

Day/Date: __________ Praying for: ______________________________

Fulfilled? ❒ Date fulfilled: ______________________

Prayer request: ____

____

____

____

____

Day/Date: __________ Praying for: ______________________________
Fulfilled? ❒ Date fulfilled: ______________________

Prayer request: ____

____

____

____

____

Day/Date: __________ Praying for: ______________________________
Fulfilled? ❒ Date fulfilled: ______________________

Prayer request: ____

____

____

____

____

Day/Date: __________ Praying for: ______________________________
Fulfilled? ❒ Date fulfilled: ______________________

Prayer request: ____

____

____

____

____

Day/Date: ___________ Praying for: ___________________________________

Fulfilled? ❒ Date fulfilled: _________________________

Prayer request: ____

____

____

____

____

Day/Date: ___________ Praying for: ___________________________________

Fulfilled? ❒ Date fulfilled: _________________________

Prayer request: ____

____

____

____

____

Day/Date: ___________ Praying for: ___________________________________

Fulfilled? ❒ Date fulfilled: _________________________

Prayer request: ____

____

____

____

____

Day/Date: __________ Praying for: ______________________________
Fulfilled? ❒ Date fulfilled: ______________________

Prayer request: ____

____

____

____

____

Day/Date: __________ Praying for: ______________________________
Fulfilled? ❒ Date fulfilled: ______________________

Prayer request: ____

____

____

____

____

Day/Date: __________ Praying for: ______________________________
Fulfilled? ❒ Date fulfilled: ______________________

Prayer request: ____

____

____

____

____

ABOUT THE AUTHORS

THOM S. RAINER is the founder and CEO of Church Answers. With nearly forty years of ministry experience, Thom has spent a lifetime committed to the growth and health of the local church and its leaders. He has been a pastor of four churches and interim pastor of ten churches, as well as a bestselling author, popular speaker, professor, and dean. He is a 1977 graduate of the University of Alabama and earned his MDiv and PhD degrees from The Southern Baptist Theological Seminary. Rainer has written numerous books, including three that ranked as number one bestsellers: *I Am a Church Member*, *Autopsy of a Deceased Church*, and *Simple Church*. He and his wife live in Franklin, Tennessee.

ASHLEY WIERSMA is a freelance writer of Christian living and spiritual memoir books and small group curricula. She and her family live in the foothills of Colorado.